The Simple Index

An Index of Biblical Topic Sub-headings

ISBN 1-889949-06-X

Published by VisionQuest
Louisville, Kentucky

The Simple Index

Three versions of the Bible are incorporated to create the **Simple Index**. Dates come from the Modern Language Bible, entries which have lower case letters after the first word are taken from the Revised Standard Version and the entries having capital letters for most words in the subheading come from the New International Version. There are a few places where this standard doesn't fit. In those cases the letters N, M and R are used to denote the version that the subheading came from. N for the NIV, M for the Modern Language and R for the Revised Standard. Please note that the words *A* and *The* have been dropped as the first word from all entries; i.e., ***The creation*** is listed as Creation; or ***A Blind Beggar*** is listed as Blind Beggar . Also, if there is a duplicate entry from both the Revised Standard and the New International one entry was dropped from the list.

Abbreviations Used

Genesis - Gen	Nahum - Nah
Exodus - Ex	Habakkuk - Hab
Leviticus - Lev	Zephaniah - Zep
Numbers - Num	Haggai - Hag
Deuteronomy - Deu	Zechariah - Zec
Joshua - Jos	Malachi - Mal
Judges - Jud	Matthew - Mat
Ruth - Ruth	Mark - Mark
1 Samuel - 1 Sam	Luke - Luke
2 Samuel - 2 Sam	John - John
1 Kings - 1 Kng	Acts - Acts
2 Kings - 2 Kng	Romans - Rom
1 Chronicles - 1 Chr	1 Corinthians - 1 Cor
2 Chronicles - 2 Chr	2 Corinthians - 2 Cor
Ezra - Ezra	Galatians - Gal
Nehemiah - Neh	Ephesians - Eph
Esther - Est	Philippians - Plip
Job - Job	Colossians - Col
Psalms - Psm	1 Thessalonians - 1 Ths
Proverbs - Pvb	2 Thessalonians - 2 Ths
Ecclesiastes - Ecc	1 Timothy - 1 Tim
Song of Solomon - Song	2 Timothy - 2 Tim
Isaiah - Isa	Titus - Titus
Jeremiah - Jer	Philemon - Plem
Lamentations - Lam	Hebrews - Heb
Ezekiel - Eze	James - Jam
Daniel - Dan	1 Peter - 1 Pet
Hosea - Hos	2 Peter - 2 Pet
Joel - Joel	1 John - 1 John
Amos - Amos	2 John - 2 John
Obadiah - Obd	3 John - 3 John
Jonah - Jon	Jude - Jude
Micah - Mic	Revelation - Rev

Topical Subheadings

SUBJECT	LOCATION
1002 B.C.	1 Chr 15:1
1002 to 995 B.C.	2 Sam 8:1
1003 B.C.	2 Sam 3:1
1003 B.C.	1 Chr 11:1
1003-1002 B.C.	1 Chr 13:1
1005 to 995 B.C.	2 Sam 21:15
1010 B.C.	2 Sam 2:1
1010 B.C.	1 Chr 10:1
1011 B.C.	1 Chr 12:1
1050 B.C.	1 Sam 10:17
1070 B.C.	1 Sam 7:1
1078-1070 B.C.	Jud 12:13
1086-1079 B.C.	Jud 12:8
1090 B.C.	1 Sam 4:1
1092-1086 B.C.	Jud 11:30
1092-1086 B.C.	Jud 12:1
1095 B.C.?	Jud 14:1
1095-1075 B.C.	Jud 15:1
1110-1070 B.C.	Jud 13:1
1133-1110 B.C.	Jud 10:1
1136 B.C.	Jud 8:29
1136-1133 B.C.	Jud 9:1
1183-1176 B.C.	Jud 6:1
1223-1183 B.C.	Jud 5:1
1323-1243 B.C.	Jud 3:15
1341-1323 B.C.	Jud 3:12
1358 B.C.	Jud 21:1
1360 B.C.	Jud 19:1
1360 B.C.?	Jud 20:1
1394 B.C.	Jos 24:1
1394-1390 B.C.	Jud 1:1
1395 B.C.	Jos 23:1
1396 B.C.	Jos 20:1
1397-1396 B.C.	Jos 19:1
1398-1397 B.C.	Jos 18:1
1399 B.C.	Jos 13:1

1399-1398 B.C.	Jos 16:1
1400 B.C.	1 Chr 6:50
1404-1403 B.C.	Jos 11:1
1405-1404 B.C.	Jos 10:38
1406 B.C.	Jos 1:1
1406-1405 B.C.	Jos 9:1
144,000 Sealed	Rev 7:1
1445 B.C.	Num 2:1
1876 B.C.	Gen 42:1
1885 B.C.	Gen 41:1
1887 B.C.	Gen 40:1
1898 B.C.	Gen 37:1
1908 B.C.	Gen 33:18
1909 B.C.	Gen 31:1
1929 B.C.	Gen 27:1
2026 B.C.	Gen 24:1
2029 B.C.	Gen 23:1
2066 B.C.	Gen 21:1
2081 B.C.	Gen 16:1
2091 B.C.	Gen 12:1
2091 B.C.?	Gen 14:1
432 B.C.	Neh 13:1
458 B.C.	Ezra 7:1
482 B.C.	Est 1:1
516 B.C.	Ezra 6:19
520 B.C.	Ezra 5:1
520-516 B.C.	Ezra 6:13
521 B.C.	Dan 9:1
534 B.C.	Ezra 4:24
535-534 B.C.	Ezra 4:1
536-535 B.C.	Ezra 3:7
537 B.C.	Ezra 2:1
537-536 B.C.	Ezra 3:1
538 B.C.	2 Chr 36:22
538 B.C.	Dan 5:1
538-537 B.C.	Ezra 1:1
539 B.C.	Dan 11:1
544 B.C.	Dan 10:1
581 B.C.	Jer 41:1
582 B.C.	2 Kng 25:22
586 B.C.	2 Kng 25:1

586 B.C.	2 Chr 36:17
586 B.C.	Jer 39:1
586-581 B.C.	Jer 40:1
587 B.C.	Jer 30:1
587 B.C.	Jer 32:1
588 B.C.	Jer 21:1
588 B.C.	Jer 34:1
588-586 B.C.	Jer 37:1
591 B.C.	Eze 8:1
592 B.C.	Eze 1:1
593 B.C.	Jer 23:1
593 B.C.	Jer 28:1
593 B.C.	Jer 50:1
597 B.C.	2 Kng 24:5
597 B.C.	2 Chr 36:9
597 B.C.	Jer 10:1
597 B.C.	Jer 17:1
597 B.C.	Jer 22:20
597 B.C.	Jer 27:1
597 B.C.	Jer 31:1
597 B.C.	Jer 35:1
603 B.C.	Jer 14:1
603 B.C.	Dan 2:1
604 B.C.	Jer 25:1
604 B.C.	Jer 36:1
604 B.C.	Jer 45:1
604-597 B.C.	Jer 16:1
605 B.C.	Jer 13:1
605 B.C.	Jer 49:1
605 B.C.	Dan 1:1
607 B.C.	Jer 7:1
607 B.C.	Jer 26:1
608 B.C.	2 Kng 23:31
608 B.C.	2 Chr 35:20
608 B.C.	Jer 22:1
608 B.C.	Jer 22:13
608-597 B.C.	Jer 9:1
609 B.C.	Jer 8:1
609 B.C.	Jer 22:10
620 B.C.	2 Chr 35:1
620 B.C.	Jer 11:1

621 B.C.	2 Chr 34:8
621 B.C.	Jer 2:14
626 B.C.	Jer 1:1
626-621 B.C.	Jer 2:1
627 B.C.	2 Chr 34:4
631 B.C.	2 Chr 34:3
639 B.C.	2 Kng 22:1
639 B.C.	2 Chr 34:1
641 B.C.	2 Kng 21:19
641 B.C.	2 Chr 33:21
696 B.C.	2 Kng 21:1
696 B.C.	2 Chr 33:1
701 B.C.	2 Chr 32:1
711 B.C.	2 Chr 32:24
713 B.C.	2 Kng 20:1
725 B.C.	2 Kng 18:1
725 B.C.	2 Chr 29:1
732 B.C.	2 Kng 15:30
736 B.C.	2 Chr 28:1
742 B.C.	2 Kng 15:23
743 B.C.	2 Kng 16:1
751 B.C.	2 Chr 26:16
752 B.C.	2 Kng 15:16
753 B.C.	2 Kng 15:8
790 B.C.	2 Kng 15:1
790 B.C.	2 Chr 25:17
791 B.C.	2 Kng 14:23
796 B.C.	2 Kng 14:1
796 B.C.	2 Chr 25:1
814 B.C.	2 Kng 10:34
835 B.C.	2 Kng 12:1
835 B.C.	2 Chr 23:1
841 B.C.	2 Kng 9:1
841 B.C.	2 Chr 22:1
848 B.C.	2 Chr 21:1
850 B.C.	2 Kng 6:1
852 B.C.	1 Kng 22:41
852 B.C.	2 Kng 1:1
853 B.C.	1 Kng 22:34
853 B.C.	2 Chr 18:1
857-856 B.C.	1 Kng 20:1

872-869 B.C.	2 Chr 17:1
872-870 B.C.	2 Chr 16:12
874 B.C.	1 Kng 16:29
885 B.C.	1 Kng 16:15
894 B.C.	2 Chr 16:1
895 B.C.	2 Chr 15:1
909 B.C.	1 Kng 15:31
910 B.C.	1 Kng 15:9
910 B.C.	2 Chr 14:1
913 B.C.	1 Kng 15:1
913 B.C.	2 Chr 13:1
926 B.C.	2 Chr 12:1
930 B.C.	1 Kng 12:1
930 B.C.	2 Chr 10:1
946 B.C.	2 Chr 8:1
950 B.C.	1 Kng 9:10
959 B.C.	1 Kng 8:1
960 B.C.	2 Chr 5:1
966 B.C.	2 Chr 3:1
970 B.C.	2 Sam 23:1
971-970 B.C.	1 Chr 23:1
983-979 B.C.	2 Sam 15:1

Ā

Aaron makes a golden calf	Ex 32:1
Aaron to speak for Moses	Ex 6:28
Aaronic benediction	Num 6:22
Abiathar banished; Joab killed	1 Kng 2:26
Abigail hears of Nabal's refusal	1 Sam 25:14
Abigail pacifies David	1 Sam 25:23
Abijah King of Judah	1 Kng 15:1
Abijah King of Judah	2 Chr 13:1
Abijah's death foretold	1 Kng 14:1
Abijah's prophecy about Jeroboam	1 Kng 11:26
Abijam, king of Judah	1 Kng 15:1
Abimelech	Jud 9:1
Abimelech made king at Shechem	Jud 9:1
Abimelech quells the revolt	Jud 9:34
Abimelech takes Abraham's wife	Gen 20:1
Abimelech's apology to Abraham	Gen 20:8

Abimelech's death in battle	Jud 9:50
Abner and Ish-bosheth quarrel	2 Sam 3:1
Abner and Joab declare a truce	2 Sam 2:24
Abner Goes Over to David	2 Sam 3:6
Abner kills Asahel	2 Sam 2:18
Abner visits David	2 Sam 3:17
About 1100 B.C.	1 Sam 1:1
About 1350 B.C.	Jud 17:1
About 899 B.C.	2 Chr 14:9
About 955 B.C.	1 Chr 19:1
About 975 B.C.	2 Sam 24:1
About 979 B.C.	2 Sam 17:1
About 990 B.C.	2 Sam 13:1
About 993 B.C.	2 Sam 12:1
About 994 B.C.	1 Chr 20:1
About 995 B.C.	2 Sam 10:1
About 995 B.C.	1 Chr 21:1
Abraham and Abimelech	Gen 20:1
Abraham and Abimelech's covenant	Gen 21:22
Abraham and the three visitors	Gen 18:1
Abraham Born 2166 B.C.	1 Chr 1:28
Abraham Justified by Faith	Rom 4:1
Abraham married Keturah	Gen 25:1
Abraham Pleads for Sodom	Gen 18:16
Abraham pleads for Sodom	Gen 18:22
Abraham saved by faith	Rom 4:1
Abraham Tested	Gen 22:1
Abraham's sacrifice of Isaac	Gen 22:9
Abram and Hagar	Gen 16:1
Abram and Lot Separate	Gen 13:1
Abram delivers Lot	Gen 14:13
Abram goes to Egypt	Gen 12:10
Abram in Egypt	Gen 12:10
Abram Rescues Lot	Gen 14:1
Absalom comes to Jerusalem	2 Sam 16:15
Absalom flees to Geshur	2 Sam 13:34
Absalom killed by Joab	2 Sam 18:9
Absalom Kills Amnon	2 Sam 13:23
Absalom living in Jerusalem	2 Sam 14:25
Absalom murders Amnon	2 Sam 13:23
Absalom Returns to Jerusalem	2 Sam 14:1

Absalom's Conspiracy	2 Sam 15:1
Absalom's Death	2 Sam 18:1
Absalom's revolt against David	2 Sam 15:1
Abundant pardon	Isa 55:6
Abuse of the concubine	Jud 19:22
Accusation of treachery	Jos 22:13
Achan's Sin	Jos 7:1
Achish Sends David Back to Ziklag	1 Sam 29:1
Acknowledgment of disgrace	Lam 5:1
Acknowledgment of past mercies	Psm 44:1
Acknowledgment of Philippian gifts	Plip 4:10
Acts requiring a sin offering	Lev 5:1
Adam and Eve	Gen 2:4
Administration of justice	Deu 17:1
Admonition for the Priests	Mal 2:1
Admonition to hold the true faith	Jude 17
Adonijah put to death	1 Kng 2:13
Adonijah seeks to be king	1 Kng 1:5
Adonijah Sets Himself Up as King	1 Kng 1:1
Adultery	Mat 5:27
Adultery and divorce	Mat 5:27
Advancement Is Meaningless	Ecc 4:13
Adversaries of Judah	Ezra 4:1
Advice About Widows, Elders and Slaves	1 Tim 5:1
Advice and instruction	Pvb 19:18
Advice of Hushai and Ahithophel	2 Sam 16:15
Advise of the false prophets	2 Chr 18:4
Aeneas and Dorcas	Acts 9:32
After calamity, restoration	Isa 32:9
Against Assyria	Zep 2:13
Against Cush	Zep 2:12
Against Judah	Zep 1:4
Against Moab and Ammon	Zep 2:8
Against Philistia	Zep 2:4
Age of the patriarchs	Acts 7:9
Agreement of the People	Neh 9:38
Ahab and Elijah meet	1 Kng 18:17
Ahab Becomes King of Israel	1 Kng 16:29
Ahab covets Naboth's vineyard	1 Kng 21:1
Ahab Defeats Ben-Hadad	1 Kng 20:13
Ahab judged for sparing Ben-hadad	1 Kng 20:35

Ahab Killed at Ramoth Gilead	1 Kng 22:29
Ahab Killed at Ramoth Gilead	2 Chr 18:28
Ahab spares Ben-hadad	1 Kng 20:30
Ahab's agreement with Jehoshaphat	1 Kng 22:1
Ahab's bargain with Jehoshaphat	2 Chr 18:1
Ahab's defeat and death	1 Kng 22:29
Ahab's Family Killed	2 Kng 10:1
Ahab's first Syrian campaign	1 Kng 20:1
Ahab's seventy sons beheaded	2 Kng 10:1
Ahab, king of Israel	1 Kng 16:29
Ahasu-erus chooses Esther	Est 2:12
Ahaz King of Judah	2 Kng 16:1
Ahaz King of Judah	2 Chr 28:1
Ahaziah flees and is killed	2 Kng 9:27
Ahaziah inquires of Baal-zebub	2 Kng 1:1
Ahaziah King of Israel	1 Kng 22:51
Ahaziah King of Judah	2 Kng 8:25
Ahaziah King of Judah	2 Chr 22:1
Ahijah's Prophecy Against Jeroboam	1 Kng 14:1
Ahimelech and the holy bread	1 Sam 21:1
Ahithophel advises to pursue David	2 Sam 17:1
Ai Destroyed	Jos 8:1
Aiming for Perfection	Psm 101:1 M
All classes to be punished	Isa 3:1
All Israel Will Be Saved	Rom 11:25
Allegory interpreted	Eze 17:11
Allegory of Abraham	Gal 4:21
Allegory of the boiling pot	Eze 24:1
Allegory of the cedar of Lebanon	Eze 31:1
Allegory of the eagles and the cedar	Eze 17:1
Allegory of the lion	Eze 19:1
Allegory of the ship, Tyre	Eze 27:1
Allegory of the two sticks	Eze 37:15
Allegory of the vine	Eze 19:10
Alliance against Joshua	Jos 11:1
Allotment for Asher	Jos 19:24
Allotment for Benjamin	Jos 18:11
Allotment for city and the prince	Eze 48:15
Allotment for Dan	Jos 19:40
Allotment for Ephraim and Manasseh	Jos 16:1
Allotment for Issachar	Jos 19:17

Allotment for Joshua	Jos 19:49
Allotment for Judah	Jos 15:1
Allotment for Naphtali	Jos 19:32
Allotment for other tribes	Eze 48:23
Allotment for priests and Levites	Eze 48:8
Allotment for Simeon	Jos 19:1
Allotment to Manasseh	Jos 17:1
Altar	Eze 43:13
Altar by the Jordan	Jos 22:7
Altar of Burnt Offering	Ex 27:1
Altar of burnt offering	Ex 29:38
Altar of burnt offering	Ex 38:1
Altar of incense	Ex 30:1
Altar of incense	Ex 37:25
Altar of sacrifice	Gen 8:20
Altar on Mount Ebal	Deu 27:1
Altar rebuilt	Ezra 3:1
Amalekites Defeated	Ex 17:8
Amalekites raid Ziklag	1 Sam 30:1
Amaziah King of Judah	2 Kng 14:1
Amaziah King of Judah	2 Chr 25:1
Ambition of James and John	Mat 20:20
Ambition of James and John	Mark 10:35
Ammonites defeated	1 Sam 11:1
Amnon and Tamar	2 Sam 13:1
Amnon defiles Tamar	2 Sam 13:1
Amon King of Judah	2 Kng 21:19
Amon King of Judah	2 Chr 33:21
An Allegory of Unfaithful Jerusalem	Eze 16:1
An altar erected in Mount Ebal	Jos 8:30
An altar on Ornan's threshing floor	1 Chr 21:18
An appeal for a holy life	1 Pet 1:13
An appeal for endurance	Heb 12:12
An Appeal for Fair Judges	Psm 58:1 M
An Appeal for Fairness	Psm 43:1 M
An appeal for God to avenge	Psm 94:1
An appeal for love and labor	1 Ths 4:9
An appeal for purity	1 Ths 4:1
An appeal for unity	1 Cor 1:10
An Appeal to God as Judge	Psm 28:1 M
An Army of Locusts	Joel 2:1

An Axhead Floats	2 Kng 6:1
An epileptic boy healed	Mat 17:14
An exhortation to trust God	Psm 146:1
An Exodus Memorial	Psm 114:1 M
An Eye for an Eye	Mat 5:38
An honest ministry	2 Cor 4:1
An Illustration From Marriage	Rom 7:1
An Invasion of Locusts	Joel 1:2
An oracle about Ethiopia	Isa 18:1
An oracle about Jehoiakim	Jer 22:18
An oracle about Jerusalem	Isa 22:1
An oracle about Philistia	Isa 14:28
An oracle about Shallum	Jer 22:10
An oracle about the king's house	Jer 22:1
An oracle about Tyre	Isa 23:1
An Oracle Against Damascus	Isa 17:1
An oracle against Shebna	Isa 22:15
An unclean spirit cast out	Luke 9:37
Analogy of family and church	Eph 5:21
Ananias and Sapphira	Acts 5:1
Ananias and Sapphira punished	Acts 5:1
Ananias restores Paul's sight	Acts 9:10
Andrew and Peter follow Jesus	John 1:35
Angel and the Little Scroll	Rev 10:1
Angel Michael	Rev 12:7
Angel of the LORD at Bokim	Jud 2:1
Angel warns Balaam	Num 22:31
Angelic messages	Rev 14:6
Angels and the shepherds	Luke 2:8
Anger and reconciliation	Mat 5:21
Anger of the LORD	Num 14:10
Anna gives thanks to God	Luke 2:36
Anointing of Jesus at Bethany	Mat 26:6
Anointing of Jesus at Bethany	Mark 14:3
Anointing of priests	Lev 8:1
Anointing Oil	Ex 30:22
Answer of the LORD	Jer 32:26
Anxiety and God's kingdom	Mat 6:25
Apollos' preaching at Ephesus	Acts 18:24
Apostles Heal Many	Acts 5:12
Apostles imprisoned	Acts 5:17

Apostles of Christ	1 Cor 4:1
Apostles Persecuted	Acts 5:17
Appeal against return to bondage	Gal 4:1
Appeal for aid against enemies	Psm 64:1
Appeal for endurance	2 Tim 2:1
Appeal for faithfulness	2 Tim 1:3
Appeal for Onesimus	Plem 8
Appeal for repentance	2 Cor 12:19
Appeal to God for deliverance	Psm 44:17
Appeal to hold firm	Heb 10:19
Appeal to rejoice in the Lord	Plip 4:1
Appeals for prayer and labor	2 Ths 3:1
Appearance beside the sea	John 21:1
Appointing of the twelve	Mark 3:13
Appointing of the Twelve Apostles	Mark 3:13
Appointment of court officials	1 Kng 4:1
Appointment of Joshua	Deu 31:1
Appointment of judges and officers	Deu 16:18
Appointment of Leaders	Deu 1:9
Appointment of musicians	1 Chr 15:16
Appointment of the seven	Acts 6:1
Appointment of the workmen	Ex 31:1
Approval of Esther	Est 9:29
April-May 966 B.C.	1 Kng 6:1
April/May, 1445 B.C.	Num 1:1
Arad Destroyed	Num 21:1
Ark	Ex 25:10
Ark	Ex 37:1
Ark and the cloud of guidance	Num 10:33
Ark Brought to Jerusalem	2 Sam 6:1
Ark Brought to Jerusalem	1 Chr 15:1
Ark Brought to the Temple	1 Kng 8:1
Ark Brought to the Temple	2 Chr 5:2
Ark in Ashdod and Ekron	1 Sam 5:1
Ark Returned to Israel	1 Sam 6:1
Ark returned to Jerusalem	2 Sam 15:24
Ark returned with sacrifices	1 Sam 6:10
Ark taken to Obed-edom	1 Chr 13:1
Armies and commerce of Tyre	Eze 27:10
Armor of God	Eph 6:10
Army Divisions	1 Chr 27:1

Around 1100 B.C.	Ruth 1:1
Arrangement of the Tribal Camps	Num 2:1
Arrangements for gatekeepers	1 Chr 26:1
Arrangements for music	1 Chr 25:1
Arrangements for treasuries	1 Chr 26:20
Arrest of Stephen	Acts 6:8
Arrival at Jerusalem	Ezra 8:31
Arrival at Rome	Acts 28:17
Artaxerxes Sends Nehemiah to Jerusalem	Neh 2:1
Asa defeats Zerah	2 Chr 14:9
Asa King of Judah	1 Kng 15:9
Asa King of Judah	2 Chr 14:2
Asa's alliance with Ben-hadad	2 Chr 16:1
Asa's Last Years	2 Chr 16:1
Asa's Reform	2 Chr 15:1
Asa's reform movement	2 Chr 15:8
Asa's sickness and death	2 Chr 16:11
Asa, king of Judah	2 Chr 14:1
Ascension	Luke 24:50
Ascension	Acts 1:6
Asher	1 Chr 7:30
Ashore on Malta	Acts 28:1
Ask, Seek, Knock	Mat 7:7
Assembling of the tabernacle	Ex 40:1
Assembly in Jerusalem	Ezra 10:9
Assignment of the cities	Jos 21:8
Assurance in the LORD	Psm 27:1 M
Assurance of the resurrection	1 Cor 15:20
Assyria, the LORD's Instrument	Isa 8:1
Assyria, the rod, to be destroyed	Isa 10:5
Assyrian alliance defeated	1 Chr 19:10
Assyrian threats	2 Kng 18:19
At Mount Sinai	Ex 19:1
At the Home of Martha and Mary	Luke 10:38
At the Potter's House	Jer 18:1
Athaliah and Joash	2 Kng 11:1
Athaliah and Joash	2 Chr 22:10
Athaliah, queen of Judah	2 Kng 11:1
Atonement for an Unsolved Murder	Deu 21:1
Atonement Money	Ex 30:11
Attack and defeat of Gog	Eze 38:14

Attempts to seize Elijah	2 Kng 1:9
August, 1407 B.C.	Num 21:1
August, 1445 B.C.	Num 13:1
Authority of Jesus Questioned	Mat 21:23
Authority of Jesus Questioned	Mark 11:27
Authority of Jesus Questioned	Luke 20:1
Azariah King of Judah	2 Kng 15:1

B

Baasha King of Israel	1 Kng 15:33
Babylon a desolation	Jer 51:24
Babylon a heap of ruins	Jer 51:34
Babylon overthrown by the Medes	Isa 13:17
Babylon's false security	Isa 47:8
Babylon's idols and the LORD	Isa 46:1
Babylon, God's Sword of Judgement	Eze 21:1
Baker's dream	Gen 40:16
Balaam visits Balak	Num 22:36
Balaam's ass speaks	Num 22:21
Balaam's Donkey	Num 22:21
Balaam's Final Oracles	Num 24:20
Balaam's first blessing	Num 22:41
Balaam's First Oracle	Num 23:1
Balaam's fourth blessing	Num 24:15
Balaam's Fourth Oracle	Num 24:15
Balaam's second blessing	Num 23:13
Balaam's Second Oracle	Num 23:13
Balaam's third blessing	Num 23:25
Balaam's Third Oracle	Num 23:27
Balak Summons Balaam	Num 22:1
Balak's anger at Balaam	Num 24:10
Baptism and Genealogy of Jesus	Luke 3:21
Baptism and Temptation of Jesus	Mark 1:9
Baptism of Jesus	Mat 3:13
Baptism of Jesus	Luke 3:21
Barak defeats Sisera	Jud 4:11
Bargain of Judas Iscariot	Mat 26:14
Bargain of Judas Iscariot	Mark 14:10
Barnabas and Saul Sent Off	Acts 13:1
Barnabas and the church at Antioch	Acts 11:19

Barren fig tree	Mat 21:18
Barren fig tree	Mark 11:12
Bartimaeus receives his sight	Mark 10:46
Basin for Washing	Ex 30:17
Basis of true knowledge	2 Pet 1:12
Basis of vindication	Psm 26:1
Basket of Ripe Fruit	Amos 8:1
Bathsheba and Nathan	1 Kng 1:15
Battle Against the Ammonites	1 Chr 19:1
Battle by the Merom	Jos 11:6
Battle in Ephraim forest	2 Sam 18:6
Be Holy	1 Pet 1:13
Beast from the earth	Rev 13:11
Beast from the sea	Rev 13:1
Beast out of the Earth	Rev 13:11
Beast out of the Sea	Rev 13:1b
Beatitudes	Mat 5:1
Beatitudes and woes	Luke 6:20
Beauty of God's Church	Psm 48:1 M
Before the Sanhedrin	Mat 26:57
Before the Sanhedrin	Mark 14:53
Before the Sanhedrin	Acts 22:30
Beginning	Gen 1:1
Beginning of Elisha's ministry	2 Kng 2:12
Beginning of Jesus' ministry	Mat 4:12
Beginning of Jesus' ministry	Mark 1:14
Beginning of Jesus' ministry	Luke 4:14
Believer's Freedom	1 Cor 10:23
Believers are the temple of God	2 Cor 6:14
Believers dead to sin	Rom 6:1
Believers Share Their Possessions	Acts 4:32
Believers' Prayer	Acts 4:23
Beloved	Song 1:2 N
Beloved	Song 1:4c N
Beloved	Song 1:12 N
Beloved	Song 1:16 N
Beloved	Song 2:1 N
Beloved	Song 2:3 N
Beloved	Song 2:16 N
Beloved	Song 4:16 N
Beloved	Song 5:2 N

Beloved	Song 5:10 N
Beloved	Song 6:2 N
Beloved	Song 7:9 N
Beloved	Song 8:5b N
Beloved	Song 8:10 N
Beloved	Song 8:14 N
Beloved Answers	Song 6:2 M
Beloved calls	Song 8:13
Beloved Calls for Her Lover	Song 4:16 M
Beloved offers his love	Song 4:8
Beloved Speaks of Her Lover	Song 2:7 M
Beloved's Refrain	Song 3:5 M
Beloved's response	Ecc 5:1a
Belshazzar summons Daniel	Dan 5:10
Belshazzar's feast	Dan 5:1
Ben-Hadad Attacks Samaria	1 Kng 20:1
Ben-hadad defeated	1 Kng 20:23
Benediction	2 Ths 3:16
Benediction	Heb 13:20
Benediction	Jude 24
Benefits of the LORD	Psm 103:1
Benjamin	1 Chr 7:6
Benjamin's birth: Rachel's death	Gen 35:16
Benjamin's two victories	Jud 20:18
Benjaminites muster their men	Jud 20:12
Besiegers encouraged	Jer 6:6
Bezalel and Oholiab	Ex 31:1
Bezalel and Oholiab	Ex 35:30
Bildad	Job 8:1
Bildad	Job 18:1
Bildad	Job 25:1
Bildad calls Job a hypocrite	Job 8:1
Bildad reproves Job	Job 18:1
Binding of Satan	Rev 20:1
Birth of a nation	Isa 66:5
Birth of Esau and Jacob	Gen 25:19
Birth of Isaac	Gen 21:1
Birth of Jesus	Mat 1:18
Birth of Jesus	Luke 2:1
Birth of Jesus Christ	Mat 1:18
Birth of Jesus Foretold	Luke 1:26

Birth of John the Baptist	Luke 1:57
Birth of John the Baptist Foretold	Luke 1:5
Birth of Moses	Ex 2:1
Birth of Samson	Jud 13:1
Birth of Samson	Jud 13:21
Birth of Samuel	1 Sam 1:1
Birth of Seth	Gen 4:25
Birth of Solomon	2 Sam 12:24
Birth of the Messianic king	Isa 9:1
Blasphemer Stoned	Lev 24:10
Blemished Sacrifices	Mal 1:6
Blessed Righteous	Psm 112:1 M
Blessing and a curse	Deu 11:26
Blessing for the night watch	Psm 134:1
Blessing of wisdom	Pvb 3:1
Blessings and Woes	Luke 6:17
Blessings for a Defiled People	Hag 2:10
Blessings for God's People	Joel 3:17
Blessings for obedience	Lev 26:1
Blessings for Obedience	Deu 28:1
Blessings of obedience	Deu 28:1
Blessings through the servant	Isa 54:1
Blessings under the Messiah	Isa 4:2
Blind and dumb healed	Mat 9:27
Blind Bartimaeus Receives His Sight	Mark 10:46
Blind Beggar Receives His Sight	Luke 18:35
Blind man of Beth-saida healed	Mark 8:22
Blind Syrians led to Samaria	2 Kng 6:20
Blood of Christ	Heb 9:11
Boasting About Tomorrow	Jam 4:13
Boaz and Ruth marry	Ruth 4:7
Boaz gives grain to Ruth	Ruth 3:14
Boaz Marries Ruth	Ruth 4:1
Boaz provides for Ruth	Ruth 2:8
Boaz recognized as their kin	Ruth 2:17
Book of the Law Found	2 Kng 22:1
Book of the Law Found	2 Chr 34:14
Boundaries of Canaan	Num 34:1
Boundaries of Judah	Jos 15:1
Boundaries of the Land	Eze 47:13
Boy Jesus at the Temple	Luke 2:41

Boy Jesus in the temple	Luke 2:41
Branch From Jesse	Isa 11:1
Branch of the LORD	Isa 4:2
Branch out of Jesse	Isa 11:1
Bread Upon the Waters	Ecc 11:1
Breastpiece	Ex 28:15
Breastpiece	Ex 39:8
Bribing of the soldiers	Mat 28:11
Bricks Without Straw	Ex 5:1
Bride and Groom to Each Other	Song 8:13 M
Bringing Back the Ark	1 Chr 13:1
Bringing the ark to Jerusalem	2 Sam 6:1
Bringing the ark to the temple	2 Chr 5:2
Bronze Snake	Num 21:4
Brother Who Sins Against You	Mat 18:15
Brotherly love	Psm 133:1 M
Brotherly unity	Psm 133:1
Budding of Aaron's rod	Num 17:1
Budding of Aaron's Staff	Num 17:1
Builders of the Wall	Neh 3:1
Building of the tabernacle	Ex 35:1
Building of the walls finished	Neh 6:15
Burden of suffering	Psm 38:1
Burden of the LORD	Jer 23:33
Burial of Gog's multitudes	Eze 39:1
Burial of Jesus	Mat 27:57
Burial of Jesus	Mark 15:42
Burial of Jesus	John 19:38
Buried in the Promised Land	Jos 24:28
Burning of the scroll	Jer 36:20
Burnt offering	Ex 29:15
Burnt Offering	Lev 1:1
Burnt Offering	Lev 6:8
Burnt offering for Job	Job 42:7
Burnt offerings	2 Chr 8:12
Butler's dream	Gen 40:9
By Faith	Heb 11:1

C

c. 4 B.C.	Mat 2:1

c. 4 B.C.	Luke 2:22
c. 5 B.C.	Mat 1:1
c. 5 B.C.	Luke 1:24
c. 6 B.C.	Luke 1:5
c. A.D. 26	Mat 3:1
c. A.D. 26	Mark 1:4
c. A.D. 26	Luke 3:1
c. A.D. 26	John 1:15
c. A.D. 27	Mark 1:9
c. A.D. 27	John 1:29
c. A.D. 28	Mark 1:14
c. A.D. 28	Luke 4:14
c. A.D. 28	John 4:1
c. A.D. 29	Mark 6:14
c. A.D. 29	Luke 9:10
c. A.D. 29	John 6:1
c. A.D. 30	Mark 10:17
c. A.D. 30	John 11:1
c. A.D. 30	Acts 1:9
c. A.D. 30-31	Acts 2:44
c. A.D. 31-32	Acts 4:31
c. A.D. 32-33	Acts 5:33
c. A.D. 36-37	Acts 6:11
c. A.D. 37	Acts 8:9
c. A.D. 37-40	Acts 9:19b
c. A.D. 40	Acts 9:26
c. A.D. 41	Acts 11:1
c. A.D. 43	Acts 11:25
c. A.D. 44	Acts 12:1
c. A.D. 47	Acts 13:1
c. A.D. 48	Acts 14:1
c. A.D. 49	Acts 14:27
c. A.D. 50	Acts 15:1
c. A.D. 51	Acts 17:1
c. A.D. 51-53	Acts 18:1
c. A.D. 53	Acts 18:12
c. A.D. 54	Acts 18:23
c. A.D. 58	Acts 20:4
c. A.D. 60	Acts 25:1
c. A.D. 61	Acts 28:7
c. A.D. 62-63	Acts 1:1

c. A.D. 8	Luke 2:41
Cain and Abel	Gen 4:1
Cain kills Abel	Gen 4:8
Cain's children	Gen 4:17
Caleb receives Hebron	Jos 14:6
Caleb Son of Hezron	1 Chr 2:18
Caleb's inheritance	Jos 15:13
Calf worship at Bethel and Dan	1 Kng 12:25
Call for national repentance	Zec 1:1
Call of Abram	Gen 12:1
Call of Elisha	1 Kng 19:19
Call of Jeremiah	Jer 1:1
Call of Levi	Luke 5:27
Call of the first disciples	Luke 5:1
Call to Build the House of the LORD	Hag 1:1
Call to God for help	Psm 77:1
Call to God for help	Psm 80:1 R
Call to Persevere	Heb 10:19
Call to Persevere	Jude 17
Call to praise the LORD	Psm 95:1 R
Call to rebuild the temple	Hag 1:1
Call to rejoice	Zep 3:14
Call to repent	Hos 14:1
Call to repent and turn from idols	Eze 14:1
Call to repentance	1 Sam 7:3
Call to Repentance	Joel 1:13
Call to repentance	Joel 2:12
Call to repentance	Amos 5:4
Call to repentance	Zep 2:1
Call to Return to the LORD	Zec 1:1
Call to trust in the LORD	Isa 31:6
Call to wait for the LORD	Zep 3:8
Call to wisdom	Pvb 8:1
Call to worship the LORD	Psm 96:1 R
Calling of Levi	Mark 2:13
Calling of Levi	Luke 5:27
Calling of Matthew	Mat 9:9
Calling of the First Disciples	Mat 4:18
Calling of the First Disciples	Mark 1:14
Calling of the First Disciples	Luke 5:1
Calling upon God in distress	Psm 18:1

21

Calm in His Friendship	Psm 62:1 M
Camp sanitation in wartime	Deu 23:9
Camps and tribal leaders	Num 2:1
Canaan cursed; Shem blessed	Gen 9:20
Captive Israel Longs to Return and See Zion Avenged	Psm 137:1 M
Capture of Jerusalem	2 Sam 5:6
Capture of Rabbah	1 Chr 20:1
Care for life and land	Pvb 12:9
Carrying out the death penalty	Deu 21:22
Cause of unbelief	John 12:36b
Causing to Sin	Mark 9:42
Cavalry from the Eu-phrates	Rev 9:13
Cedar in Lebanon	Eze 31:1
Census	Num 1:1
Census of Israel and Judah	2 Sam 24:1
Census of the people	Num 1:1
Centurion's servant healed	Mat 8:5
Centurion's servant healed	Luke 7:1
Ceremony of atonement	Lev 16:1
Certainties of faith	1 John 5:13
Certainty of doom	Jer 11:18
Certainty of God's Promise	Heb 6:13
Challenge from Assyria	Isa 37:8
Character and conduct of deceivers	2 Pet 2:10b
Character and doom of false teachers	Jude 5
Charge Against Israel	Hos 4:1
Charge to preach sound doctrine	2 Tim 4:1
Children and Parents	Eph 6:1
Children and possessions destroyed	Job 1:13
Children of Abraham	John 8:31
Children of God	1 John 2:28
Children of the Devil	John 8:42
Children to be taught commandments	Deu 11:18
Choice of a king	Deu 17:14
Choice of leaders	Deu 1:9
Choosing of the Seven	Acts 6:1
Choosing of the twelve	Luke 6:12
Choosing the better	Ecc 7:1
Chorus	Song 2:15 M
Christ our cornerstone	1 Pet 2:4

Christ our example	Heb 12:1
Christ our great example	1 Pet 2:21
Christ superior to Moses	Heb 3:1
Christ the basis of our salvation	Rom 5:12
Christ the full expression of God	Col 1:15
Christ the High Priest	Heb 2:10
Christ the once-for-all sacrifice	Heb 9:23
Christ the power and wisdom of God	1 Cor 1:18
Christ the revelation of God	Heb 1:1
Christ the Son of God	Heb 1:3b
Christ the way of approach to God	Heb 4:14
Christ the Wisdom and Power of God	1 Cor 1:18
Christ's Sacrifice Once for All	Heb 10:1
Christ, the foundation	1 Cor 3:10
Christian and persecution	1 Pet 3:13
Christian and suffering	1 Pet 4:12
Christian and the state	1 Pet 2:13
Christian and unbelievers	1 Pet 2:11
Christian conduct in review	1 Pet 3:8
Christian doctrine and conduct	Titus 2:1
Christian family	Col 3:18
Christian in the end times	1 Pet 4:1
Christian life in God's care	1 Pet 5:1
Christian rights acknowledged	1 Cor 9:1
Christian rights surrendered	1 Cor 9:15
Christian struggle	Rom 7:7
Christlike Attitude	Psm 40:1 M
Church in Antioch	Acts 11:19
Church Persecuted and Scattered	Acts 8:1
Circumcising of the nation	Jos 5:2
Circumcision and presentation	Luke 2:21
Circumcision at Gilgal	Jos 5:1
Cities for the Levites	Num 35:1
Cities of Judah	Jos 15:20
Cities of Refuge	Num 35:6
Cities of refuge	Num 35:9
Cities of Refuge	Deu 4:41
Cities of Refuge	Deu 19:1
Cities of Refuge	Jos 20:1
Cities of refuge for murderers	Deu 19:1
City is seized	Jos 8:10

City named "The LORD is there"	Eze 48:30
Claims of Jesus About Himself	John 8:48
Clans of Caleb	1 Chr 2:42
Clean and Unclean	Mat 15:1
Clean and Unclean	Mark 7:1
Clean and unclean animals	Deu 14:3
Clean and Unclean Food	Lev 11:1
Clean and Unclean Food	Deu 14:1
Clean Garments for the High Priest	Zec 3:1
Cleansing From Infectious Skin Diseases	Lev 14:1
Cleansing From Mildew	Lev 14:33
Cleansing From Sin	Zec 13:1
Cleansing of lepers	Lev 14:1
Cleansing of the temple	Mat 21:12
Cleansing of the temple	Luke 19:45
Cleansing of the temple	John 2:13
Closing advice	Deu 30:11
Closing instruction, benediction	Titus 3:12
Cloud Above the Tabernacle	Num 9:15
Cloud of guidance	Num 9:15
Collection for God's People	1 Cor 16:1
Collectors, singers and gatekeepers	Neh 12:44
Comfort and hope from God	Hag 2:1
Comfort for God's People	Isa 40:1
Comfort for the Contrite	Isa 57:14
Comfort in the resurrection hope	1 Ths 4:13
Coming apostasy	2 Tim 3:1
Coming day of the LORD	Isa 13:9
Coming day of the LORD	Joel 2:1
Coming day of the LORD	Mal 4:4
Coming Destruction	Jer 10:17
Coming of a prophet	Jud 6:7
Coming of Jethro	Ex 18:1
Coming of law and peace	Mic 4:1
Coming of the king announced	Zec 9:1
Coming of the kingdom	Luke 17:20
Coming of the Kingdom of God	Luke 17:20
Coming of the Lord	1 Ths 4:13
Coming of the rain	1 Kng 18:41
Coming of the Son of man	Mat 24:29
Coming of the Son of man	Mark 13:24

Coming of the Spirit	John 16:4b
Coming of the wise men	Mat 2:1
Coming of Timothy and Epaphroditus	Plip 2:19
Coming of Titus and the messengers	2 Cor 8:16
Coming of Zion's King	Zec 9:9
Coming ruler and his reign	Mic 5:1
Coming war and deliverer	Isa 8:1
Command concerning the unclean	Num 5:1
Command to be holy	Lev 20:22
Command to build the ark	Gen 6:9
Command to fill the ark	Gen 7:1
Command to Leave Horeb	Deu 1:1
Command to love God	Deu 11:1
Command to obtain wisdom	Pvb 4:1
Command to trust the LORD	Isa 8:16
Commended ministry	2 Cor 3:1 R
Commendation for Demetrius	3 John 11
Commendations and greetings	Rom 16:1
Commission to confinement	Eze 3:22
Commission to eat the scroll	Eze 2:8
Commission to go to Israel	Eze 2:1
Commission to speak God's message	Eze 3:4
Common Destiny for All	Ecc 9:1
Community of possessions	Acts 4:32
Community of the believers	Acts 2:37
Comparing the wicked and righteous	Psm 37:12
Compassion for the repentant	Isa 57:14
Compassion of Jerusalem	Zec 12:10
Complaint about poverty and famine	Neh 5:1
Complaint of the tribe of Joseph	Jos 17:14
Complaint over a devastated land	Psm 74:1
Completing Glorification	Psm 150:1 M
Completion and Dedication of the Temple	Ezra 6:13
Completion of the Wall	Neh 6:15
Concern for enemy and stranger	Job 31:29
Concern for the slave and the needy	Job 31:13
Concluding appeal	2 Pet 3:14
Concluding benediction	Eph 6:21
Concluding benediction	Plip 4:21
Concluding Exhortations	Heb 13:1
Concluding message	1 Cor 16:13

Concluding Remarks	1 John 5:13
Conclusion	1 Ths 5:23
Conclusion	2 John 12
Conclusion	3 John 13
Conclusion and benediction	1 Pet 5:12
Conclusion of the Matter	Ecc 12:9
Condemnation of idolatry	Isa 57:1
Conduct amidst trial	Psm 141:1
Conduct in relation to God	Rom 12:1
Conduct in relation to men	Rom 12:9
Conduct in relation to neighbors	Rom 13:8
Conduct in relation to the church	Rom 12:3
Conduct in relation to the state	Rom 13:1
Conduct in the day of salvation	Rom 13:11
Confide in God	Psm 56:1 M
Confidence facing the enemy	Psm 3:1
Confidence in the law	Psm 119:73
Confidence in the LORD	Psm 11:1 M
Confidence in the LORD's Protection	Psm 61:1 M
Conflict between north and south	Dan 11:1
Conquest of southern Canaan	Jos 10:1
Conquest of the north completed	Jos 11:16
Conquest of the south completed	Jos 10:28
Conquests by Judah and Simeon	Jud 1:1
Consecrating the priests	Ex 29:1
Consecration of the Firstborn	Ex 13:1
Consecration of the people	Ex 19:9
Consecration of the Priests	Ex 29:1
Consecration of the temple	2 Chr 29:20
Consequences of deception	2 Pet 2:17
Consequences of Israel's apostasy	Jer 2:14
Consider His wondrous works	Job 37:14
Consolation of Divine Protection	Psm 121:1 M
Conspiracy against Daniel	Dan 6:1
Construction of the ark	Ex 37:1
Contrast of the wise and the wicked	Pvb 4:10
Contrasts of wealth and poverty	Pvb 19:1
Contribution for the poor	1 Cor 16:1
Contributions for Worship	2 Chr 31:2
Controversy with the Jews	John 8:48
Conversion of Lydia	Acts 16:11

Conversion of Samaritans	John 4:39
Conversion of Saul	Acts 9:1
Conversion of Simon the sorcerer	Acts 8:9
Conversion of the Ethiopian	Acts 8:26
Conversion of the Philippian jailer	Acts 16:25
Conversion of Zacchaeus	Luke 19:1
Converts multiplied	Acts 5:12
Cooking Pot	Eze 24:1
Cornelius Calls for Peter	Acts 10:1
Cornelius sends for Peter	Acts 10:17
Cornelius' vision	Acts 10:1
Corruption of Israel	Mic 6:9
Cost of Being a Disciple	Luke 14:25
Cost of Following Jesus	Mat 8:18
Cost of Following Jesus	Luke 9:57
Council at Jerusalem	Acts 15:1
Council's Letter to Gentile Believers	Acts 15:22
Counsel and warnings	2 John 4
Counsel for the king's presence	Pvb 25:1
Counsel of despair	Mic 7:1
Counsel of Gamali-el	Acts 5:33
Counsel to a son	Pvb 24:13
Counsel to the unmarried	1 Cor 7:25
Counsel to widows	1 Cor 7:39
Count on God	Psm 37:1 M
Courageous ministry	2 Cor 5:1 R
Course of this age	Mat 24:1
Course of this age	Mark 13:1
Course of this age	Luke 21:5
Court of the tabernacle	Ex 27:9
Court of the tabernacle	Ex 38:9
Courtyard	Ex 27:9
Courtyard	Ex 38:9
Covenant between Jacob and Laban	Gen 31:43
Covenant Confirmed	Ex 24:1
Covenant Is Broken	Jer 11:1
Covenant of Circumcision	Gen 17:1
Covenant of David and Jonathan	1 Sam 20:12
Covenant of peace	Eze 34:25
Covenant renewed	Lev 26:40
Covenant Renewed at Mount Ebal	Jos 8:30

Covenant Renewed at Shechem	Jos 24:1
Covenant with Abram	Gen 15:1
Covenant with Noah	Gen 9:8
Creation	Gen 1:1
Creation of woman	Gen 2:18
Crippled Woman Healed on the Sabbath	Luke 13:10
Crossing completed	Jos 4:15
Crossing the Jordan	Jos 3:1
Crossing the Jordan on dry land	Jos 3:14
Crossing the Red Sea	Ex 14:21
Crowds Follow Jesus	Mark 3:7
Crown for Joshua	Zec 6:9
Crowning of Joshua	Zec 6:1
Crucifixion	Mat 27:32
Crucifixion	Mark 15:21
Crucifixion	Luke 23:26
Crucifixion	John 19:16b
Crucifixion and resurrection foretold	Mat 20:17
Crucifixion and resurrection foretold	Mark 10:32
Crucifixion and resurrection foretold	Luke 18:31
Crushing of Damascus and Ephraim	Isa 17:1
Cry for help continued	Psm 109:20
Cry for salvation	Psm 119:145 R
Cry for vengeance	Lam 3:55 R
Cry of An Afflicted Soul	Psm 102:1 M
Cry of anguish	Psm 22:1 R
Cry of desolation	Nah 2:10
Cry of Distress of Oppressive Neighbors	Psm 120:1 M
Cry of the Persecuted People	Psm 129:1 M
Cry to God for help	Psm 109:1 R
Cup of God's Wrath	Jer 25:15
Cup of the LORD's Wrath	Isa 51:17
Cup of the wine of wrath	Jer 25:15
Cupbearer and the Baker	Gen 40:1
Cure of Naaman the leper	2 Kng 5:1
Curse of the serpent	Gen 3:14
Curse on man and woman	Gen 3:16
Curses for Disobedience	Deu 28:15
Curses From Mount Ebal	Deu 27:9
Curses of disobedience	Deu 28:15
Curses upon the wicked	Psm 109:6

Curtain and coverings made	Ex 36:8
Custom of the priests	1 Sam 2:12
Cyrus Helps the Exiles to Return	Ezra 1:1
Cyrus promises end of exile	2 Chr 36:22
Cyrus to restore Jerusalem	Isa 44:24

D

Daily burnt offering	Num 28:1
Daily Offerings	Num 28:1
Dance before the king	Song 7:1
Daniel announces God's Judgement	Dan 5:17
Daniel delivered from the lions	Dan 6:19
Daniel detected, tried, sentenced	Dan 6:10
Daniel gives thanks to God	Dan 2:20
Daniel in the Den of Lions	Dan 6:1
Daniel Interprets the Dream	Dan 2:24
Daniel interprets the dream	Dan 2:31
Daniel's Dream of Four Beasts	Dan 7:1
Daniel's Prayer	Dan 9:1
Daniel's prayer for the people	Dan 9:1
Daniel's Training in Babylon	Dan 1:1
Daniel's Vision of a Man	Dan 10:1
Daniel's Vision of a Ram and a Goat	Dan 8:1
Daniel's vision of an angel	Dan 10:1
Danites Settle in Laish	Jud 18:1
Darius acknowledges Daniel's God	Dan 6:25
Darius' search and reply	Ezra 6:1
Date of writing: c. A.D. 48-50, probably at Jerusalem	Jam 1:1
Date of writing: c. A.D. 51, at Corinth	1 Ths 1:1
Date of writing: c. A.D. 51-52, at Corinth	2 Ths 1:1
Date of writing: c. A.D. 52-55	Gal 1:1
Date of writing: c. A.D. 56-57, at Ephesus	1 Cor 1:1
Date of writing: c. A.D. 57 in Macedonia	2 Cor 1:1
Date of writing: c. A.D. 60, at Rome	Plip 1:1
Date of writing: c. A.D. 60, at Rome	Plem 1:1
Date of writing: c. A.D. 60-61, at Rome	Eph 1:1
Date of writing: c. A.D. 60-61, at Rome	Col 1:1
Date of writing: c. A.D. 64	1 Tim 1:1
Date of writing: c. A.D. 65	Titus 1:1

Date of writing: c. A.D. 65, at Babylon	1 Pet 1:1
Date of writing: c. A.D. 65-85	1 John 1:1
Date of writing: c. A.D. 65-85	2 John 1
Date of writing: c. A.D. 65-85	3 John 1
Date of writing: c. A.D. 66-67	2 Pet 1:1
Date of writing: c. A.D. 67, at Rome	2 Tim 1:1
Date of writing: c. A.D. 68	Heb 1:1
Date of writing: c. A.D. 68	Jude 1
Date of writing: c. A.D. 95	Rev 1:1
Daughters of Jerusalem ask	Song 5:9
Daughters of Jerusalem ask	Song 6:1
Daughters of Jerusalem ask	Song 8:5a
Daughters of Jerusalem call	Song 6:13a
Daughters of Jerusalem reply	Song 1:8
Daughters of Jerusalem speak	Song 5:1b
Daughters of Zelophehad	Num 27:1
David Again Spares Saul's Life	1 Sam 26:1
David Among the Philistines	1 Sam 27:1
David and Bathsheba	2 Sam 11:1
David and Goliath	1 Sam 17:1
David and his household flee	2 Sam 15:13
David and Jonathan	1 Sam 20:1
David and Jonathan meet at Naioth	1 Sam 20:1
David and Jonathan's covenant	1 Sam 23:15
David and Mephibosheth	2 Sam 9:1
David and the Ammonites	1 Chr 19:1
David and the ark of the LORD	Psm 132:1
David and Ziba	2 Sam 16:1
David Anointed King Over Judah	2 Sam 2:1
David asks Nabal for food	1 Sam 25:1
David at Adullam and Mizpah	1 Sam 22:1
David at Gath	1 Sam 21:10
David at Keilah	1 Sam 23:1
David at Nob	1 Sam 21:1
David Becomes King Over Israel	2 Sam 5:1
David Becomes King Over Israel	1 Chr 11:1
David blesses Barzillai	2 Sam 19:31
David Builds an Altar	2 Sam 24:18
David challenges Goliath	1 Sam 17:41
David chosen to be king	1 Sam 16:6
David Conquers Jerusalem	2 Sam 5:6

David Conquers Jerusalem	1 Chr 11:4
David consults the ephod	1 Sam 30:7
David Counts the Fighting Men	2 Sam 24:1
David dances before the LORD	2 Sam 6:12
David dancing before the ark	1 Chr 15:25
David decides for Solomon	1 Kng 1:28
David Defeats the Ammonites	2 Sam 10:1
David Defeats the Philistines	2 Sam 5:17
David defeats the Philistines	1 Chr 14:1
David Defeats the Philistines	1 Chr 14:8
David Destroys the Amalekites	1 Sam 30:1
David escapes to Gath	1 Sam 21:8
David faces a choice	2 Sam 24:10
David Flees	2 Sam 15:13
David goes to the battlefield	1 Sam 17:12
David has Uriah killed	2 Sam 11:1
David Hears of Saul's Death	2 Sam 1:1
David in old age	1 Kng 1:1
David in Saul's Service	1 Sam 16:14
David invites the people to give	1 Chr 29:1
David lives with the Philistines	1 Sam 27:1
David made king of Israel	2 Sam 5:1
David Makes Solomon King	1 Kng 1:28
David marries Bathsheba	2 Sam 11:26
David marries Saul's daughter	1 Sam 18:20
David Mourns	2 Sam 18:19
David musters his men	2 Sam 17:24
David Numbers the Fighting Men	1 Chr 21:1
David plays the lyre for Saul	1 Sam 16:14
David prepares to meet Goliath	1 Sam 17:31
David repays the Gibeonites	2 Sam 21:1
David repents	2 Sam 12:7
David Returns to Jerusalem	2 Sam 19:8
David Saves Keilah	1 Sam 23:1
David smites the Amalekites	1 Sam 30:16
David spares Saul	1 Sam 24:1
David spares Saul again	1 Sam 26:6
David Spares Saul's Life	1 Sam 24:1
David told of Absalom's death	2 Sam 18:19
David's ambassadors mistreated	2 Sam 10:1
David's census	1 Chr 21:1

David's Charge to Solomon	1 Kng 2:1
David's fight continues	1 Sam 22:1
David's House and Family	1 Chr 14:1
David's instructions to Solomon	1 Chr 28:9
David's kindness to Mephibosheth	2 Sam 9:1
David's lament	2 Sam 1:17
David's Lament for Saul and Jonathan	2 Sam 1:17
David's last words	2 Sam 23:1
David's last words and death	1 Kng 2:1
David's might men	1 Chr 11:10
David's Mighty Men	2 Sam 23:8
David's Mighty Men	1 Chr 11:10
David's military victories	2 Sam 8:1
David's Officials	2 Sam 8:15
David's Officials	1 Chr 18:14
David's Plans for the Temple	1 Chr 28:1
David's Prayer	2 Sam 7:18
David's Prayer	1 Chr 17:16
David's Prayer	1 Chr 29:10
David's psalm of gratitude	1 Chr 16:7
David's psalm of praise	2 Sam 22:1
David's Psalm of Thanks	1 Chr 16:7
David's raids	1 Sam 27:8
David's Reign, 1010-970 B.C.	1 Chr 3:1
David's sin against Uriah	2 Sam 11:1
David's song of confidence	Psm 27:1
David's Song of Praise	2 Sam 22:1
David's supporters	1 Chr 12:1
David's Trust in a Self-Revealing God	Psm 86:1 M
David's Victories	2 Sam 8:1
David's Victories	1 Chr 18:1
David, king of Israel	1 Chr 11:1
David, Nabal and Abigail	1 Sam 25:1
Dawn of Zion's glory	Isa 60:1
Day and Hour Unknown	Mat 24:36
Day and Hour Unknown	Mark 13:32
Day of Atonement	Lev 16:1
Day of atonement	Lev 16:29
Day of atonement	Lev 23:26
Day of Atonement	Num 29:7
Day of atonement offerings	Num 29:7

Day of Disaster	Jer 16:1
Day of Judgement	Mal 2:17
Day of the LORD	Isa 2:6
Day of the LORD	Joel 2:28
Day of the LORD	Amos 5:18
Day of the LORD	Mal 4:1
Day of the Lord	2 Pet 3:1
Day of Wrath	Zep 1:14
Days of fulfillment at hand	Eze 12:17
Days of ordination	Lev 8:30
Days of the mighty men	Gen 6:1
Dead Are Judged	Rev 20:11
Dead Girl and a Sick Woman	Mat 9:18
Dead Girl and a Sick Woman	Mark 5:21
Dead Girl and a Sick Woman	Luke 8:40
Dead to Sin, Alive in Christ	Rom 6:1
Deaf-mute healed	Mark 7:31 R
Dealing with false doctrine	1 Tim 4:1
Dealing with false teachers	Titus 1:10
Death and burial of Joshua	Jud 2:6
Death and burial of Moses	Deu 34:1
Death and burial of Sarah	Gen 23:1
Death and resurrection foretold again	Mat 17:24
Death and resurrection foretold again	Mark 9:30
Death and resurrection foretold again	Luke 9:43b
Death for blasphemy	Lev 24:10
Death in the Pot	2 Kng 4:38
Death of Aaron	Num 20:22
Death of Abraham	Gen 25:1
Death of Abraham	Gen 25:7
Death of Amaziah	2 Kng 14:17
Death of Athaliah	2 Chr 23:12
Death of David	1 Chr 29:26
Death of Egyptian cattle	Ex 9:1
Death of Eli	1 Sam 4:12
Death of Elisha	2 Kng 13:14
Death of Ezekiel's wife	Eze 24:15
Death of Herod	Acts 12:18
Death of Isaac	Gen 35:27
Death of Jacob	Gen 49:28
Death of Jacob	Gen 49:29

Death of Jehoash	2 Kng 14:15
Death of Jehoiada and his son	2 Chr 24:15
Death of Jehoram	2 Chr 22:1
Death of Jehoshaphat	2 Chr 20:31
Death of Jeroboam	1 Kng 14:17
Death of Jesus	Mat 27:45
Death of Jesus	Mark 15:33
Death of Jesus	Luke 23:44
Death of Jesus	John 19:28
Death of Jezebel	2 Kng 9:30
Death of John the Baptist	Mat 14:1
Death of John the Baptist	Mark 6:14
Death of John the Baptist	Luke 9:7
Death of Joseph	Gen 50:22
Death of Joshua	Jos 24:29
Death of Josiah	2 Kng 23:28
Death of Josiah	2 Chr 35:20
Death of Judas Iscariot	Mat 27:3
Death of Lazarus	John 11:1
Death of Moses	Deu 34:1
Death of Nadab and Abihu	Lev 10:1
Death of Samson	Jud 16:23
Death of Sarah	Gen 23:1
Death of Saul	1 Sam 31:1
Death of Solomon	1 Kng 11:41
Death of the child	2 Sam 12:15
Death of the wicked	Job 21:17
Death Through Adam, Life Through Christ	Rom 5:12
Deaths of Rachel and Isaac	Gen 35:16
Deborah	Jud 4:1
Deborah judges Israel	Jud 4:1
Deceit Is Self-Destructive	Psm 52:1 M
December, 445 B.C.	Neh 1:1
Decision of the council	Acts 15:12
Decision sent to the Gentiles	Acts 15:22
Decision to return home	Ruth 1:6
Decree is revoked	Est 8:9
Decree of Darius	Ezra 6:1
Decree to kill the Jews	Est 3:12
Dedication of the altar	Num 7:1
Dedication of the city walls	Neh 12:27

Dedication of the Temple	2 Chr 7:1
Dedication of the Wall of Jerusalem	Neh 12:27
Dedication offering	Num 7:84
Deeds of David's mighty men	2 Sam 23:8
Deeds of the wicked	Job 24:1
Defeat and death of Ahab	2 Chr 18:28
Defeat and death of Joash	2 Chr 24:23
Defeat and exile to Babylon	2 Chr 36:17
Defeat at Ai	Jos 7:1
Defeat of Amalek	Ex 17:8
Defeat of Og	Num 21:31
Defeat of Og King of Bashan	Deu 3:1
Defeat of Sihon	Num 21:21
Defeat of Sihon and Og	Num 21:21
Defeat of Sihon King of Heshbon	Deu 2:26
Defeat of the beast and false prophet	Rev 19:11
Defeat of the Midianites	Jud 7:19
Defeated People's Prayer	Psm 44:1 M
Defeats and death of Ahaz	2 Chr 28:16
Defense against Sennacherib	2 Chr 32:1
Defense of Stephen	Acts 7:1
Defense of the faith	2 Tim 3:10
Defiling of Dinah	Gen 34:1
Delight in the will of the LORD	Psm 40:1
Delilah seeks Samson's secret	Jud 16:4
Delilah's second and third attempts	Jud 16:10
Deliverance and Destruction	Mic 5:5b
Deliverance form Moab and Ammon	2 Chr 20:20
Deliverance from death	Psm 116:1
Deliverance from desert and prison	Psm 107:4
Deliverance from persecutors	Psm 70:1
Deliverance from the sea	Psm 107:23
Deliverance from the wicked	Psm 17:10
Deliverance of Believers from Persecutors	Psm 140:1 M
Deliverance of Israel	Isa 27:1
Deliverance of the sick	Psm 107:17
Deliverance of Zion	Obd 1:17
Deliverance Promised	Mic 2:12
Deliverance through righteousness	Eze 14:12
Deliverance to the distressed	Psm 31:1
Deliverance will follow repentance	Joel 2:18

Demand for a Sign	Mat 16:1
Demetrius and the riot at Ephesus	Acts 19:23
Demoniac boy cured	Mark 9:14
Demons cast out	Mat 8:28
Demons cast out	Mark 5:1
Demons cast out	Luke 8:26
Departure from Sinai	Num 10:11
Deportations	Jer 52:24
Descendants of Adam	Gen 5:1
Descendants of Esau	Gen 36:1
Descendants of Hagar	1 Chr 1:29
Descendants of Ishmael	Gen 25:12
Descendants of Jacob	Gen 46:8
Descendants of Keturah	1 Chr 1:32
Descendants of Noah's sons	Gen 10:1
Descendants of Sarah	1 Chr 1:34
Descendants of Shem	Gen 11:10
Description of manna	Num 11:4
Description of the altar	Ex 27:1
Description of the ark	Ex 25:10
Description of the Godly	Psm 15:1 M
Description of the lampstand	Ex 25:31
Description of the tabernacle	Ex 26:1
Description of the table	Ex 25:23
Description of the temple	1 Kng 6:1
Description of the veil	Ex 26:31
Deserted soul	Psm 13:1
Desire for delicacies	Pvb 23:1
Desolation of Babylon	Rev 18:21
Desolation of Jerusalem	Isa 64:8
Desolation of Jerusalem	Eze 5:5
Desolation of the inhabitants	Eze 7:14
Destruction of Jerusalem	Luke 21:20
Destruction of Jerusalem foretold	Mic 3:9
Destruction of Jerusalem lamented	Psm 79:1
Destruction of the sanctuary	Amos 9:1
Destruction of the temple	Jer 52:12
Destruction of the treacherous	Isa 33:1
Destructive power of sin	Isa 9:18
Detestable Practices	Deu 18:9
Devoted things	Lev 27:26

Dinah and the Shechemites	Gen 34:1
Disagreement Between Paul and Barnabas	Acts 15:36
Disaster Because of Idolatry	Jer 44:1
Disaster From the North	Jer 4:5
Disaster in the land	Eze 7:1
Discharges Causing Uncleanness	Lev 15:1
Disciples Rejoin Jesus	John 4:27
Disciples' Grief Will Turn to Joy	John 16:17
Discipline of knowledge	Pvb 12:1
Discord and revolt in Shechem	Jud 9:22
Discovery of the book of the law	2 Chr 34:14
Disobedience and Defeat	Jud 2:6
Disobedience of man	Gen 3:1
Disobedient generation	Heb 3:7
Distinction between good and evil	Mal 3:13
Distress and Help	Isa 33:1
Distribution of Levite cities	Jos 21:1
Distribution of the land	Deu 3:12
Dividing the Spoils	Num 31:25
Divine deliverance	2 Kng 19:35
Divine Judgement on the Wicked	Psm 64:1 M
Divine Priest-King	Psm 110:1 M
Divine promise fulfilled	Jos 21:43
Divine Security	Psm 91:1 M
Division of Land	Deu 3:12
Division of the booty	Num 31:25
Division of the land	Num 26:52
Division of the Land	Eze 45:1
Division of the Land	Eze 48:1
Division of the Land East of the Jordan	Jos 13:8
Division of the Land West of the Jordan	Jos 14:1
Division of the priests	1 Chr 24:1
Division of the Rest of the Land	Jos 18:1
Divisions in the Church	1 Cor 1:10
Divisions of Priests	1 Chr 24:1
Divorce	Mat 5:31
Divorce	Mat 19:1
Divorce	Mark 10:1
Do all to the glory of God	1 Cor 10:23
Do not be a stumbling block	Rom 14:13
Do Not Be Yoked With Unbelievers	2 Cor 6:14

Do Not Forget the LORD	Deu 8:1
Do not judge	Rom 14:1
Do Not Love the World	1 John 2:15
Do Not Worry	Mat 6:25
Do Not Worry	Luke 12:22
Doing Good to All	Gal 6:1
Doing What Is Good	Titus 3:1
Doom of Babylon announced	Rev 18:1
Doom of Egypt	Isa 19:1
Doom to the city of Jerusalem	Isa 29:1
Downfall of Haman	Est 7:1
Doxology	Rom 11:33
Doxology	Jude 24
Doxology of the book of Romans	Rom 16:25
Dragon; the mother with child	Rev 12:1
Dream explained	Dan 7:15
Dream Is Fulfilled	Dan 4:28
Dream revealed to Daniel	Dan 2:12
Driving Out the Nations	Deu 7:1
Drought and destruction in Babylon	Jer 50:35
Drought, Famine, Sword	Jer 14:1
Duties of Priests and Levites	Num 18:1
Duties of the Levites	Num 18:1
Duties of the Levites	1 Chr 23:24
Duty to a brother's widow	Deu 25:5

E

Early 1406 B.C.	Num 25:1
Early 1406 B.C.	Deu 2:21
Early 2067 B.C.	Gen 17:1
Early 588 B.C.	Eze 24:1
Earthquake	Rev 16:17
East Gate to the Outer Court	Eze 40:5
Eastern Tribes Return Home	Jos 22:1
Eating Blood Forbidden	Lev 17:1
Eating Fat and Blood Forbidden	Lev 7:22
Ebenezer stone	1 Sam 7:12
Edom Denies Israel Passage	Num 20:14
Edom refuses Israel passage	Num 20:14
Edom's destruction to be complete	Obd 1:5

Edom's sins exposed	Obd 1:10
Edomites - People of Seir	1 Chr 1:38
Egypt and Assyria worship the LORD	Isa 19:18
Egypt to be conquered	Jer 44:24
Egypt to be conquered by Assyria	Isa 20:1
Egypt's pride and desolation	Eze 29:1
Egypt's restoration and plunder	Eze 29:13
Egyptians raid Jerusalem	2 Chr 12:1
Ehud	Jud 3:12
Ehud delivers Israel from Moab	Jud 3:12
Elah King of Israel	1 Kng 16:8
Elam and Media defeat Babylon	Isa 21:1
Elders invite David back	2 Sam 19:9
Eli's Wicked Sons	1 Sam 2:12
Elihu	Job 32:1
Elihu declares his opinion	Job 32:1
Elihu rebukes Job's pride	Job 34:31
Elihu speaks for God	Job 33:1
Elihu's warning to Job	Job 36:17
Elijah and Obadiah	1 Kng 18:1
Elijah and Obadiah meet	1 Kng 18:1
Elijah casts his mantle on Elisha	1 Kng 19:19
Elijah Fed by Ravens	1 Kng 17:1
Elijah flees from Jezebel	1 Kng 19:1
Elijah Flees to Horeb	1 Kng 19:1
Elijah in the mountain cave	1 Kng 19:9
Elijah on Mount Carmel	1 Kng 18:16
Elijah pronounces doom	1 Kng 21:17
Elijah raises the widow's son	1 Kng 17:8
Elijah Taken Up to Heaven	2 Kng 2:1
Elijah warns of a plague	2 Chr 21:11
Eliphaz	Job 4:1
Eliphaz	Job 15:1
Eliphaz	Job 22:1
Eliphaz accuses Job again	Job 22:1
Eliphaz says Job condemns himself	Job 15:1
Eliphaz urges repentance	Job 22:21
Elisha assures Jehoram of victory	2 Kng 3:13
Elisha Is Jeered	2 Kng 2:23
Elisha raises the dead son	2 Kng 4:18
Elisha refuses a reward	2 Kng 5:15

Elisha strikes the Syrians blind	2 Kng 6:8
Elisha Traps Blinded Arameans	2 Kng 6:8
Employment of Hiram	1 Kng 7:13
Empty Tomb	John 20:1
Encouragement for Gaius	3 John 5
Encouragement to Baruch	Jer 45:1
Encouragement to Be Faithful	2 Tim 1:3
Encouragement to endure suffering	2 Ths 1:3
Encouragement to trust in God	Isa 51:1
Encouraging Memories	Psm 77:1 M
End Has Come	Eze 7:1
End of affliction	Nah 1:12
End of an evil man	Job 15:17
End of Jehoshaphat's Reign	2 Chr 20:31
End of the prosperous wicked	Psm 73:1
End Times	Dan 12:1
Envoys From Babylon	2 Kng 20:12
Envoys From Babylon	Isa 39:1
Ephah of iniquity	Zec 5:5
Ephod	Ex 28:6
Ephod	Ex 39:2
Ephraim	1 Chr 7:20
Ephraim's doom determined	Hos 13:12
Ephraim's doom predicted	Hos 13:1
Ephraim's pride and hypocrisy	Isa 9:8
Ephraim's sin described	Hos 12:7
Epilogue	Job 42:7
Epilogue	Rev 22:6
Epilogue: The Wife of Noble Character	Pvb 31:10
Esau learns of the trick	Gen 27:30
Esau sells his birthright	Gen 25:27
Esau's Descendants	Gen 36:1
Esau's marriage; Isaac's sorrow	Gen 26:34
Escape to Egypt	Mat 2:13
Esther made Queen	Est 2:1
Esther's background	Est 2:5
Esther's intervention	Est 5:1
Esther's Request to the King	Est 5:1
Eternal blessing for God's people	Joel 3:17
Eternal God and mortal man	Psm 90:1
Eternal sacrifice of Christ	Heb 9:11

Eternity of wisdom	Pvb 8:22
Eutychus Raised From the Dead at Troas	Acts 20:7
Everlasting God	Isa 40:27
Everlasting kingdom	Dan 7:9
Everlasting Salvation for Zion	Isa 51:1
Everything is Meaningless	Ecc 1:1
Evil scheme of Gog	Eze 38:1
Evils of idolatry	Deu 7:1
Example of Abraham	Gal 3:6
Example of Christ	Plip 1:27
Example of Edom	Isa 34:5
Example of Jesus	2 Cor 8:8
Example of Paul	Plip 3:1
Exclusion From the Assembly	Deu 23:1
Exhortation to keep the covenant	Deu 29:1
Exhortations	Plip 4:2
Exhortations to Embrace Wisdom	Pvb 1:8
Exile for the unrepentant	Jer 8:22
Exile inevitable	Amos 6:1
Exile Symbolized	Eze 12:1
Exile the result of their sins	Zec 7:8
Exodus	Ex 12:31
Exodus and wanderings	Psm 105:37
Exodus begins	Ex 12:37
Expel the Immoral Brother!	1 Cor 5:1
Explaining the law to children	Deu 6:20
Explanation of the harlot and beast	Rev 17:6b
Exploring Canaan	Num 13:1
Extent of desolation	Jer 4:23
Extent of the flood	Gen 7:17
Exultant response of the captives	Isa 52:7
Eyes to see the truth of God's law	Psm 119:17
Ezekiel a Watchman	Eze 33:1
Ezekiel as Israel's watchman	Eze 33:1
Ezekiel's Call	Eze 2:1
Ezekiel's Wife Dies	Eze 24:15
Ezra Comes to Jerusalem	Ezra 7:1
Ezra Reads the Law	Neh 8:1
Ezra's genealogy and career	Ezra 7:1
Ezra's letter from Ar-ta-xerxes	Ezra 7:11
Ezra's prayer	Neh 9:6

Ezra's Prayer About Intermarriage	Ezra 9:1
Ezra's prayer about mixed marriages	Ezra 9:1

F

Facing persecution	Mat 10:16
Fact of the resurrection	1 Cor 15:1
Failure of Israel's leaders	Isa 56:9
Faith and Deeds	Jam 2:14
Faith and works	Titus 3:1
Faith defined	Heb 11:1
Faith in action	1 John 4:1
Faith in the living Redeemer	Job 19:25
Faith in the Son of God	1 John 5:1
Faith of a Canaanite woman	Mat 15:21
Faith of a Syrophoenician Woman	Mark 7:24
Faith of Abraham and his children	Heb 11:8
Faith of Moses the deliverer	Heb 11:23
Faith of the Canaanite Woman	Mat 15:21
Faith of the Centurion	Mat 8:5
Faith of the Centurion	Luke 7:1
Faith of the early patriarchs	Heb 11:4
Faith of the Israelites and Rahab	Heb 11:29
Faith of the judges and prophets	Heb 11:32
Faith or Observance of the Law	Gal 3:1
Faith through the Son	1 John 5:6
Faith: the means of salvation	Rom 3:21
Faithful and unfaithful servants	Mat 24:45
Faithful and unfaithful servants	Luke 12:41
Faithful urged to flee	Jer 6:1
Faithfulness of the Rechabites	Jer 35:1
Fall of Babylon	Isa 47:1
Fall of Babylon	Rev 18:1
Fall of Edom predicted	Obd 1:1
Fall of Edom shows God's love	Mal 1:1
Fall of Egypt into the Pit	Eze 31:10
Fall of Jericho	Jos 5:13
Fall of Jericho	Jos 6:15
Fall of Jerusalem	2 Chr 36:15
Fall of Jerusalem	2 Kng 25:1
Fall of Jerusalem	Jer 39:1

Fall of Jerusalem	Jer 52:1
Fall of Jerusalem predicted	2 Kng 21:10
Fall of Man	Gen 3:1
Fall, 444 B.C.	Neh 11:3
False Oracles and False Prophets	Jer 23:33
False Prophet Hananiah	Jer 28:1
False Prophets	Mic 2:6
False prophets and false teachers	2 Pet 2:1
False prophets and idolaters to die	Deu 13:1
False Prophets Condemned	Eze 13:1
False prophets of peace	Jer 14:13
False prophets of Zion	Lam 2:14
False prophets to die in shame	Jer 23:9
False Religion Worthless	Jer 7:1
False rumors about Nehemiah	Neh 6:1
False shepherd described	Zec 11:15
False Teachers and Their Destruction	2 Pet 2:1
Families of Israel gathered	Jer 31:1
Families who returned from Babylon	1 Chr 9:1
Family of Aaron	1 Chr 6:49
Family of Abraham	1 Chr 1:28
Family of Asher	1 Chr 7:30
Family of Benjamin	1 Chr 7:6
Family of Benjamin	1 Chr 8:1
Family of David	1 Chr 3:1
Family of Ephraim	1 Chr 7:20
Family of Gad	1 Chr 5:11
Family of Issachar	1 Chr 7:1
Family of Judah	1 Chr 4:1
Family of Levi	1 Chr 6:1
Family of Naphtali	1 Chr 7:13
Family of Reuben	1 Chr 5:1
Family of Saul	1 Chr 9:35
Family of Simeon	1 Chr 4:24
Family of Solomon	1 Chr 3:10
Family Record of Moses and Aaron	Ex 6:13
Famine in Besieged Samaria	2 Kng 6:24
Famine in Jerusalem	Lam 4:1
Famine of the words of the LORD	Amos 8:11
Farewell and benediction	2 Cor 13:11
Fasting	Mat 6:16

Fate of the fool	Psm 14:1
Fate of the fool	Psm 53:1
Fate of the wicked	Psm 52:1
Father's witness to the Son	John 5:30
Favoritism Forbidden	Jam 2:1
Fear God	Isa 8:11
Fear of the LORD prolongs life	Pvb 10:23
Fear the LORD	Deu 10:12
Feast of booths celebrated	Neh 8:13
Feast of first fruits	Lev 23:9
Feast of Purim instituted	Est 9:16
Feast of tabernacles	Lev 23:33
Feast of Tabernacles	Num 29:12
Feast of Tabernacles	Deu 16:13
Feast of tabernacles offerings	Num 29:12
Feast of Trumpets	Lev 23:23
Feast of Trumpets	Num 29:1
Feast of trumpets offerings	Num 29:1
Feast of unleavened bread	Ex 13:3
Feast of unleavened bread	Num 28:16
Feast of Weeks	Lev 23:15
Feast of Weeks	Num 28:26
Feast of Weeks	Deu 16:9
Feasts of weeks and tabernacles	Deu 16:9
February/March, 1406 B.C.	Num 31:1
February/March, 1406 B.C.	Deu 1:1
Feeding of a Hundred	2 Kng 4:42
Feeding of the hundred men	2 Kng 4:42
Felix defers the sentence	Acts 24:22
Fellow workmen for God	1 Cor 3:1
Fellowship of the Believers	Acts 2:42
Fellowship Offering	Lev 3:1
Fellowship Offering	Lev 7:11
Festus Consults King Agrippa	Acts 25:13
Fifth day: birds and fish	Gen 1:20
Fig Tree Withers	Mat 21:18
Final charge and benediction	1 Tim 6:20
Final Greetings	1 Cor 16:19
Final Greetings	2 Cor 13:11
Final Greetings	Eph 6:21
Final Greetings	Plip 4:21

Final Greetings	Col 4:7
Final Greetings	2 Ths 3:16
Final Greetings	2 Tim 4:19
Final Greetings	1 Pet 5:12
Final Instructions	1 Ths 5:12
Final Remarks	Titus 3:12
Final Warnings	2 Cor 13:1
Fine speech and false speech	Pvb 17:1
Finished work blessed by Moses	Ex 39:32
Fire consumes Elijah's sacrifice	1 Kng 18:30
Fire consumes the burnt offerings	2 Chr 7:1
Fire devouring the deep	Amos 7:4
Fire From the LORD	Num 11:1
Fire of judgement	Isa 66:15
First day: light	Gen 1:3
First fruits (Pentecost) offerings	Num 28:26
First-born killed	Ex 12:29
First-born set apart	Ex 13:11
Firstborn Animals	Deu 15:19
Firstfruits and Tithes	Deu 26:1
Five Amorite Kings Killed	Jos 10:16
Five thousand fed	Mat 14:13
Five thousand fed	Mark 6:30
Five thousand fed	Luke 9:10
Five thousand fed	John 6:1
Flight into Egypt	Mat 2:13
Flight to Egypt	Jer 41:16
Flight to Egypt	Jer 43:1
Flood	Gen 6:1
Flood	Gen 7:11
Flying Scroll	Zec 5:1
Follow Christ's example	Rom 15:1
Follow the LORD's Commands	Deu 26:16
Folly of Atheism	Psm 53:1 M
Folly of lust and strong drink	Pvb 31:1
Folly of Opposing the LORD	Psm 94:1 M
Folly of reliance upon Egypt	Isa 31:1
Folly of striving with God	Isa 45:9
Folly of trusting riches	Psm 49:1
Folly of trying to deceive God	Isa 29:9
Folly of yielding to a harlot	Pvb 7:1

Food at consecration	Ex 29:31
Food for the sabbath	Ex 16:22
Food offered to idols	1 Cor 8:1
Food Sacrificed to Idols	1 Cor 8:1
Fool and his folly	Pvb 26:1
Fool and the wise must die	Ecc 2:12
For protection against enemies	Psm 140:1
For the shame of Israel's enemies	Psm 129:1
Forbidden pagan practices	Deu 18:9
Forbidden portions	Lev 7:22
Forbidden tree	Gen 2:15
Foreign marriages condemned	Neh 13:23
Foreigners included in the blessing	Isa 56:1
Foreigners separated from Israel	Neh 13:1
Forgiveness for the Sinner	2 Cor 2:5
Forgiveness of an offender	2 Cor 2:5
Fortunes of Jacob restored	Jer 30:18
Four Chariots	Zec 6:1
Four chariots of divine judgement	Zec 6:1
Four Horns and Four Craftsmen	Zec 1:18
Four horns and four smiths	Zec 1:18
Four Persian kings	Dan 11:1
Four thousand fed	Mat 15:32
Four thousand fed	Mark 8:1
Fourth day: moon and stars	Gen 1:14
Frailty of man	Job 14:1
Freedom defined	Gal 5:13
Freedom for Slaves	Jer 34:8
Freedom From Human Regulations Through Life With Christ	Col 2:6
Freedom in Christ	Gal 5:1
Freeing Servants	Deu 15:12
Friend Divine	Psm 41:1 M
Friends	Song 1:4b N
Friends	Song 5:1b N
Friends	Song 5:9 N
Friends	Song 6:1 N
Friends	Song 6:13a N
Friends	Song 8:5a N
Friends	Song 8:8 N
Friends and family desert Job	Job 19:13

Friends of Job	Job 2:11
Friendship and humility	Jam 4:1
Friendship of David and Jonathan	1 Sam 18:1
From Adam to Noah	Gen 5:1
From Egypt to Nazareth	Mat 2:19
From Gloom to Confidence	Psm 38:1 M
From Josiah to the captivity	2 Chr 36:1
From Philippi to Miletus	Acts 20:5
From Ram Son of Hezron	1 Chr 2:10
From Shem to Abram	Gen 11:10
Fruitfulness of the earth	Psm 104:14
Fulfilling the law of Christ	Gal 5:25
Fulfillment of God's promise	Isa 37:30
Fulfillment of the dream	Gen 41:46
Fulfillment of the Law	Mat 5:17
Fulfillment of the new covenant	Heb 9:15
Function of the law	Gal 3:19
Furnishings of the temple	2 Chr 4:1
Further Benefits of Wisdom	Pvb 3:1
Further Instructions	Col 4:2
Further Opposition to the Rebuilding	Neh 6:1
Further parables of the kingdom	Mat 13:44
Further Sayings of the Wise	Pvb 24:23
Futile search for an upright man	Jer 5:1
Futility of toil	Ecc 2:18
Future conversion of the Gentiles	Isa 45:14
Future deliverance of God's people	Isa 29:17
Future events foretold	Mat 16:21
Future events foretold	Mark 8:31
Future events foretold	Luke 9:22
Future Glory	Rom 8:18
Future Glory of Zion	Isa 54:1
Future of Jerusalem	Zep 3:1

G

Gabriel explains the vision	Dan 8:15
Gad	1 Chr 5:11
Gad Born about 1918 B.C.	1 Chr 5:11
Garments for the priesthood	Ex 28:1

Garments of the priesthood	Ex 39:1
Gatekeepers	1 Chr 26:1
Gates of the City	Eze 48:30
Gates to the Inner Court	Eze 40:28
Gedaliah appointed governor	Jer 40:7
Gedaliah Assassinated	Jer 40:7
Gedaliah murdered by Ishmael	Jer 41:1
Gedaliah, the governor, murdered	2 Kng 25:22
Gehazi's greed and punishment	2 Kng 5:19
Genealogies from Israel to David	1 Chr 2:1
Genealogies of priests and Levites	Neh 12:1
Genealogies of the patriarchial age	1 Chr 1:1
Genealogy of Abram	Gen 11:27
Genealogy of David	Ruth 4:13
Genealogy of Israel	Ex 6:14
Genealogy of Jesus	Mat 1:1
Genealogy of Jesus	Luke 3:23
Genealogy of Saul	1 Chr 9:35
Genealogy of Saul the Benjamite	1 Chr 8:1
Genealogy of those who returned	Neh 7:5
General Christian obligations	Heb 13:1
Generosity Encouraged	2 Cor 8:1
Gentiles receive the Holy Spirit	Acts 10:44
Gentiles: guilty before God	Rom 1:18
Gershonites	Num 4:21
Gershonites	1 Chr 23:7
Gethsemane	Mat 26:36
Gethsemane	Mark 14:32
Gibeonite Deception	Jos 9:1
Gibeonites Avenged	2 Sam 21:1
Gideon	Jud 6:1
Gideon called by the LORD	Jud 6:11
Gideon chooses three hundred men	Jud 7:1
Gideon Defeats the Midianites	Jud 7:1
Gideon destroys the altar of Baal	Jud 6:25
Gideon puts out the fleece	Jud 6:36
Gideon refused supplies	Jud 8:4
Gideon refuses the kingship	Jud 8:22
Gideon's Death	Jud 8:28
Gideon's death; Israel apostasy	Jud 8:29
Gideon's Ephod	Jud 8:22

Gideon's offering consumed	Jud 6:19
Gift of the Holy Spirit	Acts 2:1
Gifts for Building the Temple	1 Chr 29:1
Gifts of Prophecy and Tongues	1 Cor 14:1
Gifts of the Spirit	Eph 4:7
Giving of the Macedonians	2 Cor 8:1
Giving to the Needy	Mat 6:1
Glorification of Zion	Isa 62:6
Glorious restoration of Israel	Isa 49:22
Glory Departs From the Temple	Eze 10:1
Glory of the Holy One	Hab 3:1
Glory of the LORD	Ex 40:34
Glory of the LORD	Psm 8:1 M
Glory of the New Covenant	2 Cor 3:7
Glory of Zion	Isa 60:1
Glory Returns to the Temple	Eze 43:1
God able to foretell the future	Isa 41:21
God and Idols	Jer 10:1
God and Moses at Sinai	Deu 5:22
God announces the last plague	Ex 11:1
God blesses Noah	Gen 9:1
God Cares	Psm 34:1 M
God commissions Moses	Ex 3:7
God delivers the righteous	Psm 73:21
God Disciplines His Sons	Heb 12:1
God does great things	Job 5:8
God Equips Moses	Ex 4:1
God forbids Balaam to go to Balak	Num 22:1
God glorified in His people	Isa 66:18
God guides the nations	Psm 67:1
God hears and acts	Psm 10:12
God in the Nation's History	Psm 78:1 M
God intervenes to redeem Zion	Isa 59:15
God is just in his dealings	Job 36:1
God is not far away	Psm 38:15
God is not unjust	Job 34:1
God is witness in heaven	Job 16:18
God lets Balaam go	Num 22:15
God loves a cheerful giver	2 Cor 9:6
God of All Comfort	2 Cor 1:3
God of salvation	Psm 68:19

God of the exodus	Psm 68:1
God of the exodus	Psm 114:1
God of the mountain	Psm 68:11
God of the Nations	Psm 67:1 M
God of the sanctuary	Psm 68:24
God of the wilderness	Psm 68:7
God Our Protector	Psm 31:1 M
God Our Strength	Psm 46:1 M
God Promises Deliverance	Ex 5:22
God promises deliverance	Job 5:17
God Rejects Zedekiah's Request	Jer 21:1
God renews the covenant with Jacob	Gen 35:1
God Saves; Worship Him	Psm 98:1 M
God sees the ways of man	Job 34:16
God sends quails for meat	Num 11:31
God tests Abraham	Gen 22:1
God the author of his affliction	Job 19:8
God the creator of the earth	Psm 104:1
God the king of the earth	Psm 47:1
God the Only Helper; the Compassionate Deliverer	Psm 146:1 M
God the sustainer of life	Psm 104:24
God to be glorified in the body	1 Cor 6:9
God to purge Israel	Eze 20:32
God to regather Israel	Eze 36:22
God to send Cyrus against Babylon	Isa 48:12
God to show mercy to the obedient	Eze 20:40
God uses pain to chasten men	Job 33:19
God will defeat the nations	Deu 7:17
God will prosper Israel	Isa 41:17
God will restore Jerusalem	Isa 52:1
God's Accusation Against the Wicked	Isa 56:9
God's Angel to Prepare the Way	Ex 23:20
God's anger with Samaria and Judah	Mic 1:2
God's Answer	Jer 12:5
God's blessings upon the nation	Isa 44:1
God's Care for His Creation	Psm 104:1 M
God's Care for Israel	Psm 105:1 M
God's care of His redeemed	Isa 49:8
God's Chosen Servant	Mat 12:15
God's command to Rehoboam	1 Kng 12:21

God's compassion toward Israel	Hos 11:8
God's complaint against the people	Mic 6:1
God's Covenant With Abram	Gen 15:1
God's covenant with David	Psm 89:1
God's Covenant With Noah	Gen 9:1
God's Day of Vengeance and Redemption	Isa 63:1
God's Faithful Provision for His Covenant People	Psm 136:1 M
God's Faithfulness	Rom 3:1
God's glory and man's honor	Psm 8:1
God's glory fills the tabernacle	Ex 40:34
God's Glory in Nature and in His Word	Psm 19:1 M
God's goodness to wayward Israel	Psm 81:1
God's Great Goodness	Psm 103:1 M
God's great requirement	Deu 10:12
God's guidance of his people	Psm 78:1
God's intent to restore Jerusalem	Zec 8:1
God's judgement against Judah	Isa 5:24
God's Judgement on Assyria	Isa 10:5
God's judgement upon idol worship	Isa 44:6
God's judgement upon men	Gen 6:5
God's judgment on Eli's house	1 Sam 3:10
God's justice and mercy	Rom 9:14
God's kingdom to triumph on earth	Isa 2:1
God's knowledge and greatness	Job 11:7
God's law a hiding place	Psm 119:113
God's law a lamp to the feet	Psm 119:105
God's law is true	Psm 119:137
God's law taught by affliction	Psm 119:65
God's Love and Ours	1 John 4:7
God's Love for Israel	Hos 11:1
God's love will redeem His people	Isa 43:1
God's Mercies and Israel's Rebellion	Psm 106:1 M
God's mercies in the wilderness	Deu 8:1
God's Mercy and Israel's Unfaithfulness	Isa 43:14
God's name: I AM WHO I AM	Ex 3:13
God's oath unchanging	Heb 6:13
God's Omniscience, Omnipresence, and Omnipotence	Psm 139:1 M
God's pardon and love	Mic 7:15
God's People Rejoice in His Victory	Psm 149:1 M

God's power and deeds	Psm 66:1
God's Power and Justice	Psm 97:1 M
God's power and wisdom	Isa 40:12
God's principles of judgement	Rom 2:1
God's promise of deliverance	Ex 5:22
God's Promise to David	2 Sam 7:1
God's Promise to David	1 Chr 17:1
God's promise to the repentant	Isa 30:18
God's Promises to David	Psm 89:1 M
God's promises to David	Psm 89:19
God's provisions for the earth	Psm 65:1
God's reason for judgement	Jer 5:18
God's reply to Moses	Num 11:16
God's requirement of a holy life	Isa 1:10
God's Righteous Judgment	Rom 2:1
God's sentence	Hos 8:11
God's severity toward Israel	Hos 5:1
God's Sovereign Choice	Rom 9:1
God's unchangeable law	Psm 119:89
God's vengeance and goodness	Nah 1:1
God's ways are beyond man	Ecc 8:10
God's wisdom and might	Job 12:13
God's wonders of old	Psm 77:11
God's Wrath Against Mankind	Rom 1:18
God's years and man's days	Psm 102:23
God, His People's Protector	Psm 76:1 M
God, the hope of Israel	Jer 17:11
God, the Judge of Judges	Psm 82:1 M
God-fearing family is blessed	Psm 128:1
Godless and the upright	Pvb 11:1
Godlessness in the Last Days	2 Tim 3:1
Godly and the Ungodly	Psm 1:1 M
Gods of Babylon	Isa 46:1
Going to War	Deu 20:1
Gold Lampstand and the Two Olive Trees	Zec 4:1
Golden Calf	Ex 32:1
Golden Calf	Deu 9:7
Golden calf at Horeb	Psm 106:19
Golden calf destroyed	Deu 9:13
Golden Calves at Bethel and Dan	1 Kng 12:25
Goliath killed; the Philistines routed	1 Sam 17:50

Goliath the Philistine	1 Sam 17:1
Gomer's adultery and judgement	Hos 2:2
Gomer's restoration accomplished	Hos 3:1
Gomer's restoration promised	Hos 2:14
Good fight of faith	1 Tim 6:11
Good Samaritan	Luke 10:25
Good thoughts for bad times	Psm 12:1
Good tidings of salvation	Isa 61:1
Goodness of the LORD	Psm 145:1
Gospel offered to the Jews	Rom 9:30
Grain Offering	Lev 2:1
Grain Offering	Lev 6:14
Gratitude for Divine Rescue	Psm 30:1 M
Great Commandment	Mat 22:34
Great commandment	Mark 12:28
Great commission	Mat 28:16
Great commission	Luke 24:44
Great Day of the LORD	Zep 1:14
Great Glory of Zion	Psm 87:1 M
Great invitation	Isa 55:1
Great Multitude in White Robes	Rev 7:9
Great Suffering Followed by Deliverance	Psm 22:1 M
Great white throne judgement	Rev 20:11
Greatest Commandment	Mat 22:34
Greatest Commandment	Mark 12:28
Greatest in the kingdom	Mat 18:1
Greatest in the Kingdom of Heaven	Mat 18:1
Greatness of Modecai	Est 10:1
Greek woman's faith	Mark 7:24
Greetings and benediction	2 Tim 4:9
Greetings and benediction	Plem 23
Greetings and Doxology	Rev 1:4
Greetings and final instructions	Col 4:10
Growth of true knowledge	2 Pet 1:3
Guard at the Tomb	Mat 27:62
Guards posted along the walls	Neh 4:10
Guards' Report	Mat 28:11
Guilt of Judah	Isa 5:8
Guilt Offering	Lev 5:14
Guilt Offering	Lev 7:1
Guilty in God's presence	Isa 64:1

Habakkuk's Complaint	Hab 1:2
Habakkuk's Prayer	Hab 3:1
Habakkuk's Second Complaint	Hab 1:12
Hagar and Ishmael	Gen 16:1
Hagar and Ishmael	Gen 16:7
Hagar and Ishmael cast out	Gen 21:8
Hagar and Ishmael in the wilderness	Gen 21:15
Hagar and Ishmael Sent Away	Gen 21:8
Hagar and Sarah	Gal 4:21
Half of Manasseh settles in Gilead	Num 32:28
Half-Tribe of Manasseh	1 Chr 5:23
Hallelujah!	Rev 19:1
Haman Hanged	Est 7:1
Haman has gallows made	Est 5:9
Haman's plot against the Jews	Est 3:7
Haman's plot and its failure	Est 6:1
Haman's Plot to Destroy the Jews	Est 3:1
Haman's Rage Against Mordecai	Est 5:9
Hamites	1 Chr 1:8
Hanani and Hananiah appointed	Neh 7:1
Hanani, the seer, warns Asa	2 Chr 16:7
Handwriting on the wall	Dan 5:5
Hanging of Haman's sons	Est 9:11
Hannah Dedicates Samuel	1 Sam 1:21
Hannah's Prayer	1 Sam 2:1
Hannah's song of praise	1 Sam 2:1
Happiness of the godly	Psm 1:1
Happiness of the holy	Psm 15:1
Harvest of the Earth	Rev 14:14
Hastily-gotten inheritance	Pvb 20:15
Hatred of Saul	1 Sam 18:6
Hatred of the world	John 15:18
Hazael anointed king of Syria	2 Kng 8:7
Hazael Murders Ben-Hadad	2 Kng 8:7
He of Her	Song 8:5b M
He Speaks of Her	Song 1:15 M
He to Her	Song 2:2 M
Healing at the Pool	John 5:1
Healing of a Blind Man at Bethsaida	Mark 8:22

Healing of a Boy With an Evil Spirit	Mark 9:14
Healing of a Boy With an Evil Spirit	Luke 9:37
Healing of a Deaf and Dumb Man	Mark 7:31
Healing of a Demon-possessed Man	Mark 5:1
Healing of a Demon-possessed Man	Luke 8:26
Healing of an Epileptic Boy	Mat 17:14
Healing of the lame man	Acts 3:1
Healing of the official's son	John 4:46
Healing of the ten lepers	Luke 17:11
Healing of the Water	2 Kng 2:19
Healing of two blind men	Mat 20:29
Healing of Two Demon-possessed Men	Mat 8:28
Healing on the Sabbath	Mat 12:9
Healing the blind man near Jericho	Luke 18:35
Hear the words to the wise	Pvb 22:17
Heartfelt Praise	Psm 29:1 M
Heavenly Joy	Psm 33:1 M
Heavenly worship	Rev 4:1
Hebrew Servants	Ex 21:2
Hebrews slaves to be freed	Deu 15:12
Hebron Given to Caleb	Jos 14:6
Help for deciding disputes	Pvb 18:17
Help from the LORD	Psm 121:1
Helper of Israel	Isa 41:1
Her Appeal to Jerusalem's Maidens	Song 5:8 M
Her Beauty as She Dances	Song 6:13 M
Her Call to Her Lover	Song 7:10 M
Her Description of Her Lover	Song 5:10 M
Her Dream Song	Song 5:2 M
Her Love Song to Him	Song 2:8 M
Her Tender Wish for Him	Song 8:1 M
Heritage of the wicked	Job 20:20
Herod's Death	Acts 12:19b
Hezekiah Celebrates the Passover	2 Chr 30:1
Hezekiah cleanses the temple	2 Chr 29:3
Hezekiah King of Judah	2 Kng 18:1
Hezekiah pays tribute to Assyria	2 Kng 18:13
Hezekiah Purifies the Temple	2 Chr 29:1
Hezekiah sends to Isaiah	2 Kng 19:1
Hezekiah's appeal to God	Isa 37:1
Hezekiah's folly and exile	Isa 39:1

Hezekiah's foolishness	2 Kng 20:12
Hezekiah's Illness	2 Kng 20:1
Hezekiah's Illness	Isa 38:1
Hezekiah's praise after recovery	Isa 38:9
Hezekiah's Prayer	2 Kng 19:14
Hezekiah's Prayer	Isa 37:14
Hezekiah's prayer to the LORD	Isa 37:14
Hezekiah's prayer while sick	Isa 38:1
Hezekiah's Pride, Success and Death	2 Chr 32:24
Hezekiah's sickness and death	2 Chr 32:24
Hezekiah, king of Judah	2 Kng 18:1
Hezekiah, king of Judah	2 Chr 29:1
High places destroyed	2 Chr 31:1
High places to be destroyed	Eze 6:1
High Priest of a New Covenant	Heb 8:1
High Priest Questions Jesus	John 18:19
Higher righteousness	Mat 5:17
His death as seen by God	Isa 53:10
His death as seen by man	Isa 53:7
His request to go to Jerusalem	Neh 2:1
Historical Records From Adam to Abraham	1 Chr 1:1
Holiness and personal conduct	Lev 19:1
Holiness and uncleanness	Hag 2:10
Holy places profaned	Eze 7:23
Holy Spirit Comes at Pentecost	Acts 2:1
Honor given Jehoiachin	Jer 52:31
Hope and comfort in God's law	Psm 119:49
Hope for the remnant of Israel	Eze 11:13
Hope in God's mercies	Lam 3:19
Hope in resurrection	Isa 26:16
Horsemen among the myrtles	Zec 1:7
Hosea's marriage to Gomer	Hos 1:1
Hosea's Reconciliation With His Wife	Hos 3:1
Hosea's Wife and Children	Hos 1:2
Hoshea Last King of Israel	2 Kng 17:1
House of Jacob urged to repent	Isa 2:5
Household of God	Eph 2:11
Household provisions	1 Kng 4:22
How burnt offerings are made	Lev 6:8
How cereal offerings are made	Lev 6:14
How Great Thou Art!	Psm 65:1 M

How Great Thy Goodness!	Psm 66:1 M
How guilt offerings are made	Lev 7:1
How peace offerings are made	Lev 7:11
How sin offerings are made	Lev 6:24
How to Worship Acceptably	Psm 81:1 M
Human pride to be humbled	Isa 2:12
Humility of the apostles	1 Cor 4:1
Husband and the wife	1 Pet 3:1
Hushai advises to muster forces	2 Sam 17:1
Hymn of praise to God	Psm 113:1 R
Hymn of the exiles in Babylon	Psm 137:1 R

I

Ibzan, Elon and Abdon	Jud 12:8
Ibzan, Elon and Abdon judge Israel	Jud 12:8
Idol Feasts and the Lord's Supper	1 Cor 10:14
Idolaters Condemned	Eze 14:1
Idolaters Killed	Eze 9:1
Idolatrous cities to be destroyed	Deu 13:12
Idolatry Forbidden	Deu 4:15
Idolatry in the Temple	Eze 8:1
Idolatry in the wilderness	1 Cor 10:1
Idolatry Judah's sin	Jer 17:1
Idols and the living God contrasted	Isa 40:18
If a man die, shall he live again?	Job 14:7
Image of Gold and the Fiery Furnace	Dan 3:1
Imitating Christ's Humility	Plip 2:1
Immature reproved	Heb 5:11
Imminent horrors of invasion	Isa 17:9
In Athens	Acts 17:16
In Berea	Acts 17:10
In Corinth	Acts 18:1
In Exaltation of the LORD	Psm 93:1 M
In Her Dream She Responds	Song 5:3 M
In Her Heart She Answers Him	Song 1:16 M
In Iconium	Acts 14:1
In Lystra and Derbe	Acts 14:8
In Pisidian Antioch	Acts 13:13
In the chambers of the king	Song 1:1
In Thessalonica	Acts 17:1

In time of trouble	Psm 39:1
Incense	Ex 30:34
Indictment of Jerusalem	Eze 22:1
Inequalities of life	Ecc 9:11
Ingrafted Branches	Rom 11:11
Inheritance of Zelophehad's Daughters	Num 36:1
Innocent before God	Psm 17:1
Inquiry about extra fasts	Zec 7:1
Institution of the Passover	Ex 12:1
Instruction in wisdom	Pvb 15:21
Instructions for godly living	1 Tim 4:6
Instructions on Worship	1 Tim 2:1
Instructions to Timothy	1 Tim 4:1
Integrity of heart	Psm 101:1
Integrity of the righteous	Pvb 20:1
Interior of the temple	1 Kng 6:14
Interpretation and warning	Dan 4:19
Interpretation of the Dream	Dan 7:15
Interpretation of the Vision	Dan 8:15
Interpreting the present time	Luke 12:54
Interpreting the Times	Luke 12:54
Introduction	1 Cor 1:1
Introduction	2 Cor 1:1
Introduction	1 John 1:1
Introduction	Jude 1
Introduction of the Book of Luke	Luke 1:1
Introduction of Tychicus and Onesimus	Col 4:7
Introduction to the Law	Deu 4:44
Invader will suddenly destroy	Jer 6:22
Investment of a life	Ecc 11:1
Invitation to the Thirsty	Isa 55:1
Invitation to wisdom	Pvb 8:32
Invitations of Wisdom and of Folly	Pvb 9:1
Is Jesus the Christ?	John 7:25
Isaac and Abimelech	Gen 26:1
Isaac and Rebekah	Gen 24:1
Isaac and Rebekah marry	Gen 24:62
Isaac dwells in Gerar	Gen 26:1
Isaac quarrels with the herdsmen	Gen 26:17
Isaac sends Jacob to Laban	Gen 28:1
Isaiah brings an answer	2 Kng 19:20

Isaiah cleansed and commissioned	Isa 6:1
Isaiah Prophesies Sennacherib's Fall	2 Kng 19:20
Isaiah's Commission	Isa 6:1
Isaiah's words to Ahaz	Isa 7:1
Ish-Bosheth Murdered	2 Sam 4:1
Ish-bosheth, king of Israel	2 Sam 2:8
Ishmael routed by Johanan	Jer 41:11
Ishmael's Sons	Gen 25:12
Israel (*Jacob*) Born 2006 B.C.	1 Chr 2:1
Israel a chosen people	Deu 7:6
Israel a rebellious people	Isa 65:1
Israel appeals to Jephthah	Jud 11:1
Israel as a chosen nation	Deu 4:32
Israel Asks for a King	1 Sam 8:1
Israel becomes a harlot	Eze 16:15
Israel Blind and Deaf	Isa 42:18
Israel chooses to serve the LORD	Jos 24:16
Israel chosen of God	Isa 41:8
Israel cries for deliverance	Jud 10:10
Israel defeated by the Philistines	1 Sam 4:1
Israel defeated in battle	Deu 1:41
Israel demands a king	1 Sam 8:1
Israel Exiled Because of Sin	2 Kng 17:7
Israel fails to keep the covenant	Jud 2:1
Israel Fights the Remaining Canaanites	Jud 1:1
Israel Forsakes God	Jer 2:1
Israel Freed	Isa 48:12
Israel has drunk the cup of wrath	Isa 51:17
Israel Has Not Returned to God	Amos 4:1
Israel in Egypt	Psm 105:23
Israel in the wilderness	Acts 7:35
Israel like Sodom and Samaria	Eze 16:43b
Israel on the march	Num 21:10
Israel Punished and Restored	Hos 2:2
Israel punished for idolatry	Eze 36:16
Israel Rebels Against Rehoboam	1 Kng 12:1
Israel Rebels Against Rehoboam	2 Chr 10:1
Israel rebuilt	Eze 36:33
Israel resettled with Assyrians	2 Kng 17:24
Israel Routs the Philistines	1 Sam 14:15
Israel taken captive to Assyria	2 Kng 18:9

Israel the Chosen	Isa 44:1
Israel to be a captive of Assyria	Hos 11:1
Israel to be delivered	Isa 27:2
Israel to Be Destroyed	Amos 9:1
Israel to be returned	Eze 36:8
Israel to cross Jordan	Jos 3:1
Israel to flee Babylon	Isa 48:17
Israel to Reap the Whirlwind	Hos 8:1
Israel to return home	Jer 50:17
Israel Unrepentant	Hos 6:1
Israel weeps for Benjamin	Jud 21:1
Israel will overcome her foes	Isa 41:11
Israel Will Rise	Mic 7:8
Israel Without Weapons	1 Sam 13:16
Israel's acceptance of the covenant	Ex 24:1
Israel's adultery	Hos 4:14
Israel's apostasy	Jud 2:11
Israel's apostasy in Canaan	Eze 20:27
Israel's apostasy in Egypt	Eze 20:1
Israel's apostasy in the wilderness	Eze 20:13b
Israel's approval of the altar	Jos 22:30
Israel's confession of sins	Isa 59:9
Israel's defeat at Hormah	Num 14:39
Israel's enemies to be smitten	Isa 30:27
Israel's exile beyond Damascus	Amos 5:18
Israel's failure to return to God	Amos 4:4
Israel's faithlessness	Jer 2:1
Israel's forgetfulness	Psm 78:40
Israel's fortresses to be destroyed	Hos 10:9
Israel's fortunes to be restored	Amos 9:11
Israel's future salvation	Rom 11:11
Israel's growth and bondage	Ex 1:1
Israel's Guilt and Punishment	Mic 6:9
Israel's idolatry in Canaan	Psm 78:56
Israel's idolatry in Shittim	Num 25:1
Israel's idolatry to be punished	Jer 2:20
Israel's idols to be destroyed	Hos 10:1
Israel's immorality	Dan 4:1
Israel's ingratitude	Isa 1:2
Israel's inheritance	Psm 78:67
Israel's iniquity and intrigue	Hos 6:11

Israel's jealousy	2 Sam 19:41
Israel's Misery	Mic 7:1
Israel's Only Savior	Isa 43:1
Israel's oppressors judged	Eze 36:1
Israel's population to decline	Hos 9:10
Israel's provisions	Psm 78:17
Israel's punishment	Num 14:20
Israel's punishment; God's mercy	Psm 106:40
Israel's Rebellion Predicted	Deu 31:14
Israel's Restoration	Amos 9:11
Israel's riches to be taken away	Hos 9:1
Israel's second census	Num 26:1
Israel's sin	Hos 8:1
Israel's Sin	Hos 12:1
Israel's Sin and the Servant's Obedience	Isa 50:1
Israel's sin at the Red Sea	Psm 106:6
Israel's sin of ingratitude	Isa 43:22
Israel's sins	Psm 78:9
Israel's sins denounced	Mic 3:1
Israel's sins in Canaan	Psm 106:24
Israel's sins in the wilderness	Psm 106:13
Israel's Sons	1 Chr 2:1
Israel's ultimate deliverance	Isa 32:1
Israel's Unbelief	Rom 9:30
Israel's unfaithfulness renewed	Hos 6:4
Israel's waywardness	Psm 78:32
Israel, a maiden of beauty	Eze 16:8
Israel, an orphan child	Eze 16:1
Israel, the faithless one	Jer 3:6
Israelites Confess Their Sins	Neh 9:1
Israelites Fight the Benjamites	Jud 20:1
Israelites Leave Sinai	Num 10:11
Israelites Oppressed	Ex 1:1
Issachar	1 Chr 7:1

J

Jabesh-gilead attacked	Jud 21:8
Jacob and Esau	Gen 25:19
Jacob and Esau meet	Gen 33:1
Jacob Arrives in Paddan Aram	Gen 29:1

Jacob blesses his sons	Gen 49:1
Jacob blesses Joseph's sons	Gen 48:1
Jacob Flees From Laban	Gen 31:1
Jacob flees from Laban	Gen 31:17
Jacob Flees to Laban	Gen 27:41
Jacob Gets Isaac's Blessing	Gen 27:1
Jacob goes to Egypt	Gen 46:1
Jacob journeys to Shechem	Gen 33:15
Jacob Loved, Esau Hated	Mal 1:2
Jacob Marries Leah and Rachel	Gen 29:14
Jacob marries Leah and Rachel	Gen 29:15
Jacob Meets Esau	Gen 33:1
Jacob meets Rachel	Gen 29:9
Jacob plans to return home	Gen 31:1
Jacob prepares to meet Esau	Gen 32:1
Jacob Returns to Bethel	Gen 35:1
Jacob steals Esau's blessing from Isaac	Gen 27:18
Jacob Wrestles With God	Gen 32:22
Jacob's bargain with Laban	Gen 30:25
Jacob's burial in Canaan	Gen 50:4
Jacob's children	Gen 29:31
Jacob's dream at Bethel	Gen 28:10
Jacob's Flocks Increase	Gen 30:25
Jacob's journey	Gen 29:1
Jacob's present for Esau	Gen 32:13
Jacob's wrestling at Peniel	Gen 32:22
Jael kills Sisera	Jud 4:17
Jahaziel promises deliverance	2 Chr 20:13
Jair	Jud 10:3
Jairus' daughter raised; a suffering woman healed	Mark 5:21
James and John rebuked	Luke 9:51
James killed; Peter imprisoned	Acts 12:1
January/February, 1406 B.C.	Num 22:1
January/February, 1406 B.C.	Deu 3:1
Japhethites	1 Chr 1:5
Jehoahaz King of Israel	2 Kng 13:1
Jehoahaz King of Judah	2 Kng 23:31
Jehoahaz King of Judah	2 Chr 36:2
Jehoash King of Israel	2 Kng 13:10
Jehoash pays off Hazael	2 Kng 12:17

Jehoash repairs the temple	2 Kng 12:4
Jehoash, king of Israel	2 Kng 13:10
Jehoash, king of Judah	2 Kng 11:21
Jehoiachin in exile	2 Kng 25:27
Jehoiachin King of Judah	2 Kng 24:8
Jehoiachin King of Judah	2 Chr 36:9
Jehoiachin Released	2 Kng 25:27
Jehoiachin Released	Jer 50:31
Jehoiada overthrows Athaliah	2 Kng 11:4
Jehoiakim Burns Jeremiah's Scroll	Jer 36:1
Jehoiakim King of Judah	2 Kng 23:36
Jehoiakim King of Judah	2 Chr 36:5
Jehoram King of Judah	2 Kng 8:16
Jehoram King of Judah	2 Chr 21:4
Jehoram musters forces in Samaria	2 Kng 3:1
Jehoram's campaign against Moab	2 Kng 3:21
Jehoram, king of Judah	2 Chr 21:1
Jehoshaphat Appoints Judges	2 Chr 19:4
Jehoshaphat Defeats Moab and Ammon	2 Chr 20:1
Jehoshaphat King of Judah	1 Kng 22:41
Jehoshaphat King of Judah	2 Chr 17:1
Jehoshaphat's prayer	2 Chr 20:1
Jehoshaphat's prosperity	2 Chr 17:10
Jehoshaphat, king of Judah	2 Chr 17:1
Jehovah Praised as Restorer and Defender	Psm 147:1 M
Jehu Anointed King of Israel	2 Kng 9:1
Jehu kills Ahaziah and Ahab's kin	2 Kng 10:12
Jehu Kills Joram and Ahaziah	2 Kng 9:14
Jehu murders Ahaziah	2 Chr 22:7
Jehu tricks and kills Joram	2 Kng 9:14
Jehu's massacre of Baal worshipers	2 Kng 10:18
Jephthah	Jud 10:6
Jephthah and Ephraim	Jud 12:1
Jephthah and the Ammonite king	Jud 11:12
Jephthah's daughter sacrificed	Jud 11:34
Jephthah's quarrel with Ephraim	Jud 12:1
Jephthah's vow	Jud 11:29
Jerahmeel Son of Hezron	1 Chr 2:25
Jeremiah and Pashhur	Jer 20:1
Jeremiah arrested and released	Jer 26:1
Jeremiah Buys a Field	Jer 32:1

Jeremiah cast into the miry pit	Jer 38:1
Jeremiah complains to the LORD	Jer 20:7
Jeremiah exposes Hananiah	Jer 28:1
Jeremiah Freed	Jer 40:1
Jeremiah in Prison	Jer 37:1
Jeremiah pities himself	Jer 15:15
Jeremiah preaches, though persecuted	Jer 20:1
Jeremiah questioned by the king	Jer 37:16
Jeremiah released	Jer 40:1
Jeremiah Threatened With Death	Jer 26:1
Jeremiah Thrown Into a Cistern	Jer 38:1
Jeremiah warns of punishment	Jer 34:12
Jeremiah warns remnant not to flee	Jer 42:1
Jeremiah's advice to Zedekiah	Jer 38:17
Jeremiah's arrest and imprisonment	Jer 37:1
Jeremiah's Complaint	Jer 12:1
Jeremiah's Complaint	Jer 20:7
Jeremiah's Prayer	Jer 10:23
Jeremiah's prayer	Jer 32:16
Jeremiah's rescue from the pit	Jer 38:7
Jeroboam II King of Israel	2 Kng 14:23
Jeroboam Rebels Against Solomon	1 Kng 11:26
Jeroboam's sin continues	1 Kng 13:33
Jerusalem and the temple destroyed	2 Kng 25:8
Jerusalem delivered by the LORD	Zec 14:1
Jerusalem falls; the land desolate	Eze 33:21
Jerusalem Maidens	Song 6:1 M
Jerusalem to Be Inhabited	Isa 44:24
Jerusalem Under Siege	Jer 6:1
Jerusalem's Deliverance Foretold	2 Kng 19:1
Jerusalem's Deliverance Foretold	Isa 37:1
Jerusalem's desolation	Lam 1:1
Jerusalem's Enemies to be Destroyed	Zec 12:1
Jerusalem's Fall Explained	Eze 33:21
Jerusalem's loneliness	Lam 1:15
Jerusalem's sin	Lam 1:8
Jerusalem's Sins	Eze 22:1
Jerusalem, A Useless Vine	Eze 15:1
Jesus Again Predicts His Death	Mat 20:17
Jesus Again Predicts His Death	Mark 10:32
Jesus Again Predicts His Death	Luke 18:31

Jesus and Beelzebub	Mat 12:22
Jesus and Beelzebub	Mark 3:20
Jesus and Beelzebub	Luke 11:14
Jesus and his followers	Luke 8:1
Jesus and John the Baptist	Mat 11:1
Jesus and John the Baptist	Luke 7:18
Jesus and the little children	Luke 18:15
Jesus and the Miraculous Catch of Fish	John 21:1
Jesus and the woman of Samaria	John 4:1
Jesus Anointed at Bethany	Mat 26:6
Jesus Anointed at Bethany	Mark 14:1
Jesus Anointed at Bethany	John 12:1
Jesus Anointed by a Sinful Woman	Luke 7:36
Jesus anointed by Mary of Bethany	John 12:1
Jesus anointed by the sinful woman	Luke 7:36
Jesus answers the Pharisees	Luke 16:14
Jesus answers the Pharisees' slander	Mat 12:22
Jesus answers the Pharisees' slander	Mark 3:19b
Jesus answers the Pharisees' slander	Luke 11:14
Jesus Appears to His Disciples	John 20:19
Jesus appears to Mary Magdalene	John 20:11
Jesus Appears to Mary of Magdala	John 20:10
Jesus Appears to the Disciples	Luke 24:36
Jesus appears to the disciples	John 20:19
Jesus appears to the ten	Luke 24:36
Jesus Appears to Thomas	John 20:24
Jesus Arrested	Mat 26:47
Jesus Arrested	Mark 14:43
Jesus Arrested	Luke 22:47
Jesus Arrested	John 18:1
Jesus at a Pharisee's House	Luke 14:1
Jesus at the feast of Dedication	John 10:22
Jesus at the feast of Tabernacles	John 7:1
Jesus at the Temple	Mat 21:12
Jesus at the Temple	Luke 19:45
Jesus before Caiaphas	Mat 26:57
Jesus before Caiaphas	Mark 14:53
Jesus before Jewish authorities	John 18:12
Jesus Before Pilate	Mat 27:11
Jesus Before Pilate	Mark 15:1
Jesus Before Pilate	John 18:28

Jesus Before Pilate and Herod	Luke 22:66
Jesus before Pontius Pilate	Mat 27:11
Jesus before Pontius Pilate	Mark 15:1
Jesus before Pontius Pilate	Luke 23:1
Jesus before Pontius Pilate	John 18:28
Jesus Begins to Preach	Mat 4:12
Jesus blesses the little children	Mat 19:13
Jesus blesses the little children	Mark 10:13
Jesus calls four disciples	Mat 4:18
Jesus calls four disciples	Mark 1:16
Jesus Calls Philip and Nathanael	John 1:43
Jesus Calms the Storm	Mat 8:23
Jesus Calms the Storm	Mark 4:35
Jesus Calms the Storm	Luke 8:22
Jesus Changes Water to Wine	John 2:1
Jesus Clears the Temple	Mark 11:12
Jesus Clears the Temple	John 2:12
Jesus Comforts His Disciples	John 14:1
Jesus Comforts the Sisters	John 11:17
Jesus crowned with thorns	Mat 27:27
Jesus crowned with thorns	Mark 15:16
Jesus crowned with thorns	John 19:1
Jesus crucified	Mat 27:32
Jesus crucified	Mark 15:21
Jesus crucified	Luke 23:32
Jesus crucified	John 19:17
Jesus delivered to Pilate	Mat 27:1
Jesus dismisses Judas, his betrayer	John 13:21
Jesus Drives Out an Evil Spirit	Mark 1:21
Jesus Drives Out an Evil Spirit	Luke 4:31
Jesus Feeds the Five Thousand	Mat 14:13
Jesus Feeds the Five Thousand	Mark 6:30
Jesus Feeds the Five Thousand	Luke 9:10
Jesus Feeds the Five Thousand	John 6:1
Jesus Feeds the Four Thousand	Mat 15:29
Jesus Feeds the Four Thousand	Mark 8:1
Jesus Goes to the Feast of Tabernacles	John 7:1
Jesus Greater Than Moses	Heb 3:1
Jesus Heals a Man Born Blind	John 9:1
Jesus Heals a Paralytic	Mat 9:1
Jesus Heals a Paralytic	Mark 2:1

Jesus Heals a Paralytic	Luke 5:17
Jesus Heals Many	Mat 8:14
Jesus Heals Many	Mark 1:29
Jesus Heals Many	Luke 4:38
Jesus heals many by the sea	Mark 3:7
Jesus heals on the Sabbath	Mark 3:1
Jesus heals on the Sabbath	Luke 6:6
Jesus heals on the Sabbath	Luke 14:1
Jesus heals on the Sabbath	John 5:1
Jesus Heals the Blind and Dumb	Mat 9:27
Jesus heals the man born blind	John 9:1
Jesus Heals the Official's Son	John 4:43
Jesus Heals the Sick	Mat 4:23
Jesus hears of Lazarus' death	John 11:1
Jesus Is Coming	Rev 22:7
Jesus laid in the tomb	Mat 27:57
Jesus laid in the tomb	Mark 15:42
Jesus laid in the tomb	Luke 23:50
Jesus laid in the tomb	John 19:38
Jesus Like Melchizedek	Heb 7:11
Jesus Made Like His Brothers	Heb 2:5
Jesus on the way to Calvary	Luke 23:26
Jesus Prays for All Believers	John 17:20
Jesus Prays for Himself	John 17:1
Jesus Prays for His Disciples	John 17:6
Jesus Prays in a Solitary Place	Mark 1:35
Jesus Prays on the Mount of Olives	Luke 22:39
Jesus preaches in Galilee	Mark 1:35
Jesus Predicts His Betrayal	John 13:18
Jesus Predicts His Death	Mat 16:21
Jesus Predicts His Death	Mark 8:31
Jesus Predicts His Death	John 12:20
Jesus Predicts Peter's Denial	Mat 26:31
Jesus Predicts Peter's Denial	Mark 14:27
Jesus Predicts Peter's Denial	John 13:31
Jesus Presented in the Temple	Luke 2:21
Jesus Promises the Holy Spirit	John 14:15
Jesus Questioned About Fasting	Mat 9:14
Jesus Questioned About Fasting	Mark 2:18
Jesus Questioned About Fasting	Luke 5:33
Jesus questions Peter	John 21:15

Jesus Raises a Widow's Son	Luke 7:11
Jesus raises Lazarus	John 11:38
Jesus Raises Lazarus From the Dead	John 11:38
Jesus Reinstates Peter	John 21:15
Jesus rejected at Nazareth	Mat 13:53
Jesus rejected at Nazareth	Mark 6:1
Jesus Rejected at Nazareth	Luke 4:14
Jesus rejected at Nazareth	Luke 4:16
Jesus reveals the Father	Mat 11:25
Jesus Sends Out the Seventy-two	Luke 10:1
Jesus Sends Out the Twelve	Mat 10:1
Jesus Sends Out the Twelve	Mark 6:6b
Jesus Sends Out the Twelve	Luke 9:1
Jesus Sentenced to be Crucified	John 19:1
Jesus sought by the Gentiles	John 12:20
Jesus Taken to Annas	John 18:12
Jesus Taken Up Into Heaven	Acts 1:1
Jesus talks to the healed man	John 9:35
Jesus Talks With a Samaritan Woman	John 4:1
Jesus talks with Mary	John 11:28
Jesus Teaches at the Feast	John 7:14
Jesus Teaches Nicodemus	John 3:1
Jesus the bread of life	John 6:22
Jesus the Bread of Life	John 6:25
Jesus the divider	Luke 12:49
Jesus the good shepherd	John 10:1
Jesus the Great High Priest	Heb 4:14
Jesus the Lamb of God	John 1:29
Jesus the light of the world	John 8:12
Jesus the Lord of the Sabbath	Mat 12:1
Jesus the Lord of the Sabbath	Mark 2:23
Jesus the Lord of the Sabbath	Luke 6:1
Jesus the resurrection and the life	John 11:17
Jesus the true vine	John 15:1
Jesus the Way to the Father	John 14:5
Jesus visits Mary and Martha	Luke 10:38
Jesus walks on the sea	Mat 14:22
Jesus walks on the sea	John 6:15
Jesus Walks on the Water	Mat 14:22
Jesus Walks on the Water	Mark 6:45
Jesus Walks on the Water	John 6:16

Jesus walks the sea	Mark 6:45
Jesus warns against unbelief	John 8:21
Jesus Washes His Disciples' Feet	John 13:1
Jesus weeps over Jerusalem	Luke 19:41
Jesus' agony in Gethsemane	Mat 26:36
Jesus' agony in Gethsemane	Mark 14:32
Jesus' agony in Gethsemane	Luke 22:39
Jesus' ascension	Luke 24:50
Jesus' authority challenged	Mat 21:23
Jesus' authority challenged	Mark 11:27
Jesus' authority challenged	Luke 20:1
Jesus' betrayal and arrest	Mat 26:47
Jesus' betrayal and arrest	Mark 14:43
Jesus' betrayal and arrest	Luke 22:47
Jesus' betrayal and arrest	John 18:1
Jesus' Burial	Luke 23:50
Jesus' call to repentance	Luke 13:1
Jesus' Death	Luke 23:44
Jesus' farewell to his disciples	John 16:16
Jesus' First Disciples	John 1:35
Jesus' healing at Gennesaret	Mark 6:53
Jesus' Mother and Brothers	Mat 12:46
Jesus' Mother and Brothers	Mark 3:31
Jesus' Mother and Brothers	Luke 8:19
Jesus' Sorrow for Jerusalem	Luke 13:31
Jesus' Teaching on Prayer	Luke 11:1
Jesus' true family	Mat 12:46
Jesus' true family	Mark 3:31
Jesus' true family	Luke 8:19
Jesus' warning against the scribes	Mark 12:38
Jethro Visits Moses	Ex 18:1
Jews and the Law	Rom 2:17
Jews Continue in Their Unbelief	John 12:37
Jews dispute Jesus' claim	John 6:41
Jews oppose; Gentiles believe	Acts 13:44
Jews try to arrest Jesus	John 10:31
Jews: guilty before God	Rom 2:17
Jezebel Killed	2 Kng 9:30
Jezebel seizes the vineyard	1 Kng 21:5
Joab kills Abner	2 Sam 3:26
Joab kills Amasa	2 Sam 20:4

Joab Murders Abner	2 Sam 2:22
Joab rebukes David	2 Sam 19:1
Joab secures Absalom's return	2 Sam 14:1
Joash Repairs the Temple	2 Chr 24:1
Joash Repairs the Temple	2 Kng 12:1
Joash, king of Judah	2 Chr 24:1
Job	Job 6:1
Job	Job 9:1
Job	Job 12:1
Job	Job 16:1
Job	Job 19:1
Job	Job 21:1
Job	Job 23:1
Job	Job 26:1
Job	Job 42:1
Job acknowledges God as creator	Job 10:1
Job afflicted with sores	Job 2:7
Job again complains against God	Job 10:14
Job alleges God's anger with him	Job 16:6
Job and his background	Job 1:1
Job argues against hope	Job 7:1
Job asks for evidence of his sins	Job 6:24
Job asks why he did not die	Job 3:11
Job asserts God's greatness	Job 26:1
Job calls his friends unfaithful	Job 6:14
Job calls his friends unkind	Job 16:1
Job claims innocence	Job 9:13
Job claims to speak the truth	Job 27:1
Job cries out in his agony	Job 3:20
Job curses the day of his birth	Job 3:1
Job defends God's justice	Job 9:1
Job denies Zophar's accusations	Job 12:1
Job describes God's power	Job 12:7
Job despises the wicked	Job 27:7
Job disagrees with his friends	Job 21:27
Job is mocked and hated	Job 30:1
Job prays to God	Job 7:7
Job repents in dust and ashes	Job 42:1
Job Speaks	Job 3:1
Job submits to God's wisdom	Job 40:3
Job tormented by words	Job 19:1

Job urged to repent	Job 11:13
Job wants God to let him die	Job 6:1
Job wants to find God and be tried	Job 23:1
Job's complaint against God	Job 9:25
Job's defense of his integrity	Job 13:13
Job's earlier prosperity	Job 29:1
Job's First Test	Job 1:6
Job's fortunes restored	Job 42:10
Job's innocence and purity	Job 31:1
Job's resentment of his friends	Job 13:1
Job's Second Test	Job 2:1
Job's suffering and turmoil	Job 30:16
Job's Three Friends	Job 2:11
John eats the scroll	Rev 10:1
John the Baptist Beheaded	Mat 14:1
John the Baptist Beheaded	Mark 6:14
John the Baptist Denies Being the Christ	John 1:19
John the Baptist Prepares the Way	Mat 3:1
John the Baptist Prepares the Way	Mark 1:1
John the Baptist Prepares the Way	Luke 3:1
John the Baptist's Testimony About Jesus	John 3:22
John's testimony to Jesus	John 3:25
John's witness to himself	John 1:19
John's witness to Jesus	John 1:29
Jonah cast into the sea	Jon 1:11
Jonah Flees From the LORD	Jon 1:1
Jonah flees to Tarshish	Jon 1:1
Jonah Goes to Nineveh	Jon 3:1
Jonah preaches at Nineveh	Jon 3:1
Jonah's Anger at the LORD's Compassion	Jon 4:1
Jonah's Prayer	Jon 2:1
Jonathan and Ahima-az warn David	2 Sam 17:17
Jonathan Attacks the Philistines	1 Sam 14:1
Jonathan breaks Saul's oath	1 Sam 14:24
Jonathan Eats Honey	1 Sam 14:24
Jonathan saved by the people	1 Sam 14:43
Jonathan tries to pacify Saul	1 Sam 19:1
Jonathan's excuse for David	1 Sam 20:24
Jonathan's guilt discovered	1 Sam 14:36
Joseph and Potiphar's Wife	Gen 39:1
Joseph and the Famine	Gen 47:13

Joseph eats with his brothers	Gen 43:26
Joseph in Charge of Egypt	Gen 41:41
Joseph interprets dreams	Gen 40:1
Joseph interprets Pharaoh's dream	Gen 41:25
Joseph Makes Himself Known	Gen 45:1
Joseph meets his brothers	Gen 42:6
Joseph Reassures His Brothers	Gen 50:15
Joseph reveals his identity	Gen 45:1
Joseph Sold by His Brothers	Gen 37:12
Joseph sold to traders	Gen 37:25
Joseph wrongly cast into prison	Gen 39:19
Joseph's brothers bow before him	Gen 44:14
Joseph's Brothers Go to Egypt	Gen 42:1
Joseph's brothers return to Egypt	Gen 43:16
Joseph's brothers visit Egypt	Gen 42:1
Joseph's dream; his brothers' hatred	Gen 37:1
Joseph's Dreams	Gen 37:1
Joseph's kin invited to Egypt	Gen 45:16
Joseph's promise to Jacob	Gen 47:27
Joseph's prosperity and integrity	Gen 39:1
Joshua and the man with a sword	Jos 5:13
Joshua cleansed and reclothed	Zec 3:1
Joshua selected to succeed Moses	Num 27:12
Joshua to Succeed Moses	Num 27:12
Joshua to Succeed Moses	Deu 31:1
Joshua's address to Israel	Jos 23:1
Joshua's blessing	Jos 22:1
Joshua's Farewell to the Leaders	Jos 23:1
Joshua's last message	Jos 24:1
Josiah Celebrates the Passover	2 Chr 35:1
Josiah Renews the Covenant	2 Kng 23:1
Josiah repairs the temple	2 Kng 22:3
Josiah repairs the temple	2 Chr 34:8
Josiah's Reforms	2 Chr 34:1
Josiah, king of Judah	2 Kng 22:1
Josiah, king of Judah	2 Chr 34:1
Jotham King of Judah	2 Kng 15:32
Jotham King of Judah	2 Chr 27:1
Jotham's parable of the bramble	Jud 9:7
Journey from Egypt to Canaan	Num 33:1
Journey to Moab	Num 21:10

Joy in God's presence	Psm 16:1
Joy of Confession and Forgiveness	Psm 32:1 M
Joy of good news	2 Cor 7:5
Joy of the new age	Isa 65:17
Joy of the Redeemed	Isa 35:1
Judah - To Hezron's Sons	1 Chr 2:3
Judah and Tamar	Gen 38:1
Judah and Tamar	Gen 38:12
Judah appeals to God	Isa 63:15
Judah beyond deliverance	Jer 14:1
Judah has broken the covenant	Jer 11:1
Judah pleads for Benjamin	Gen 43:18
Judah to Serve Nebuchadnezzar	Jer 27:1
Judah Unfaithful	Mal 2:10
Judah's captivity; Babylon's end	Jer 25:1
Judah's distress; God's vengeance	Isa 33:7
Judah's idolatry and immorality	Jer 7:1
Judah's king supreme over the earth	Zec 14:9
Judah's marriage to Shua	Gen 38:1
Judah, the unfaithful wife	Jer 3:1
Judas Agrees to Betray Jesus	Mat 26:14
Judas Agrees to Betray Jesus	Luke 22:1
Judas Hangs Himself	Mat 27:1
Judgement against Babylon	Isa 47:1
Judgement Against Evil Kings	Jer 22:1
Judgement Against Israel	Hos 5:1
Judgement Against Samaria and Jerusalem	Mic 1:3
Judgement Against the Nations	Isa 34:1
Judgement and Hope	Isa 66:1
Judgement and Restoration	Eze 20:30
Judgement and Salvation	Isa 65:1
Judgement cannot be avoided	Jer 15:1
Judgement for universal sin	Isa 24:1
Judgement Inescapable	Eze 14:12
Judgement of Babylon, the harlot	Rev 17:1
Judgement of Judah's enemies	Joel 3:1
Judgement of the immoral	1 Cor 5:9
Judgement of the LORD	Isa 3:13
Judgement of the LORD	Lam 2:1
Judgement of the nations	Isa 41:1
Judgement of the unrepentant	Mat 11:20

Judgement on Israel	Amos 2:6
Judgement on Israel's Enemies	Zec 9:1
Judgement on Israel's Leaders	Eze 11:1
Judgement on Israel's Neighbors	Amos 1:3
Judgement on Jerusalem and Judah	Isa 3:1
Judgement on Oholah and Oholibah	Eze 23:36
Judgement on the nations	Isa 34:1
Judgement to come from the north	Jer 4:5
Judgement upon Israel	Eze 16:35
Judgement upon Jacob	Hos 12:2
Judgement upon Jerusalem	Zep 1:2
Judgement upon the nations	Obd 1:12
Judges	Deu 16:18
Judging and hypocrisy	Mat 7:1
Judging Others	Mat 7:1
Judging Others	Luke 6:37
Judgment	Mat 25:31
June, 1445 B.C.	Num 12:1
Justice and Mercy, Not Fasting	Zec 7:1
Justice of God	Psm 75:1
Justice of the LORD	Psm 145:13

K

Keeper's of God's law are blessed	Psm 119:1
Keeping God's law in adversity	Psm 119:153
Keeping the Sabbath Holy	Jer 17:19
Killing the Passover lamb	Ex 12:21
Killings of the Midianites	Num 31:1
King	Deu 17:14
King and his court surrender	2 Kng 24:10
King and the princes	Ecc 10:16
King Artaxerxes' Letter to Ezra	Ezra 7:11
King as priest and victor	Psm 110:1
King Chooses four Israelites	Dan 1:1
King expresses his love	Song 1:9
King offers his love	Song 4:1
King pays homage to Daniel	Dan 2:46
King returns	Song 3:6
King sets up an image	Dan 3:1
King tells his dream to Daniel	Dan 4:1

King Who Exalts Himself	Dan 11:36
King's Edict in Behalf of the Jews	Est 8:1
King's marriage	Psm 45:1
King's Overseers	1 Chr 27:25
King's punishment for pride	Dan 4:28
King's repentance and recovery	Dan 4:34
Kingdom of Righteousness	Isa 32:1
Kings assembled at Armageddon	Rev 16:12
Kings defeated east of the Jordan	Jos 12:1
Kings defeated west of the Jordan	Jos 12:7
Kings of Edom	1 Chr 1:43
Kings of Judah	1 Chr 3:10
Kings of the South and the North	Dan 11:1
Kitchens for the temple	Eze 46:19
Kohathites	Num 4:1
Kohathites	1 Chr 23:12
Korah, Dathan and Abiram	Num 16:1

L

Laban Pursues Jacob	Gen 31:22
Laish burned and rebuilt	Jud 18:27
Lamb and the 144,000	Rev 14:1
Lamb on Mount Zion	Rev 14:1
Lament and Call to Repentance	Amos 5:1
Lament for Egypt	Eze 30:1
Lament for Israel's Princes	Eze 19:1
Lament for Pharaoh	Eze 32:1
Lament for Tyre	Eze 27:1
Lament for the king of Tyre	Eze 28:11
Lament of the princes of the sea	Eze 26:15
Lament of the prophet	Mic 1:8
Lament over Babylon	Rev 18:9
Lament over Egypt	Eze 32:17
Lament over Israel	Amos 5:1
Lament over Jerusalem	Mat 23:37
Lament over Jerusalem	Luke 13:31
Lament over personal affliction	Lam 3:1
Lament over Pharaoh	Eze 32:1
Lamp of the Body	Luke 11:33
Lamp on a Stand	Mark 4:21

Lamp on a Stand	Luke 8:16
Lampstand	Ex 25:31
Lampstand	Ex 37:17
Lampstand	Num 8:1
Lampstand and two olive trees	Zec 4:1
Land allotted to the north	Eze 48:1
Land east of the Jordan	Jos 13:8
Land for priests and prince	Eze 45:1
Land of Asher	Jos 19:24
Land of Benjamin	Jos 18:11
Land of Dan	Jos 19:40
Land of Issachar	Jos 19:17
Land of Joseph	Jos 16:1
Land of Naphtali	Jos 19:32
Land of Simeon	Jos 19:1
Land of the Ephraimites	Jos 16:5
Land of the Gadites	Jos 13:24
Land of the Manassites	Jos 13:29
Land of the Reubenites	Jos 13:15
Land of Zebulun	Jos 19:10
Land policies of Joseph	Gen 47:13
Land Still to Be Taken	Jos 13:1
Land survey; casting the lots	Jos 18:1
Land yet to be conquered	Jos 13:1
Last day of the feast	John 7:37
Last Supper	Mat 26:17
Last Supper	Mark 14:12
Last Supper	Luke 22:7
Last Words of David	2 Sam 23:1
Late 1407 B.C.	Deu 2:1
Late 2067 B.C.	Gen 18:1
Later Opposition Under Artaxerxes	Ezra 4:6
Laver, oil and incense	Ex 30:17
Law about beating	Deu 25:1
Law about captive wives	Deu 21:10
Law about landmarks	Deu 19:14
Law about special sacrifices	Lev 17:1
Law about suspected adultery	Num 5:11
Law Courts	Deu 17:8
Law for a Nazirite	Num 6:1
Law of burnt offering	Lev 1:1

Law of cereal offerings	Lev 2:1
Law of clean animals	Lev 11:1
Law of eating holy food	Lev 10:12
Law of love	Lev 19:17
Law of love	Deu 6:4
Law of love	Luke 6:27
Law of money-lending	Lev 25:35
Law of peace offerings	Lev 3:1
Law of restitution	Num 5:5
Law of the guilt offering	Lev 5:14
Law of the Passover	Ex 12:43
Law of the Promise	Gal 3:15
Law of unclean animals	Lev 11:24
Law read and explained	Neh 7:73
Laws about appointed feasts	Ex 23:14
Laws about appointed feasts	Ex 34:18
Laws about divorce and marriage	Deu 24:1
Laws about human relationships	Deu 23:15
Laws about livestock	Ex 21:28
Laws about military service	Deu 20:1
Laws about murder	Ex 21:12
Laws about personal actions	Ex 22:16
Laws about priests in the temple	Eze 44:15
Laws about property	Ex 22:2
Laws about quarreling and fighting	Ex 21:18
Laws about sexual relationships	Deu 22:13
Laws about siege	Deu 20:10
Laws about skin diseases	Lev 13:1
Laws about slaves	Ex 21:1
Laws about the innocent and needy	Deu 24:16
Laws about the Sabbath	Ex 23:10
Laws about the use of the temple	Eze 44:1
Laws about the welfare of others	Deu 22:1
Laws about tithes	Deu 14:22
Laws about uncleanness in men	Lev 15:1
Laws about uncleanness in women	Lev 15:19
Laws about vows	Num 30:1
Laws about weights and measures	Deu 25:13
Laws about weights and offerings	Eze 45:10
Laws about witnesses	Deu 19:15
Laws about witnesses and ransom	Num 35:29

Laws and tests for leprosy	Lev 13:9
Laws concerning sons	Deu 21:15
Laws of Justice and Mercy	Ex 23:1
Laws of the Sabbath	Lev 23:1
Laws protecting the poor	Deu 24:6
Lawsuits Among Believers	1 Cor 6:1
Lawsuits among brothers	1 Cor 6:1
Lazy man and the lying tongue	Pvb 26:13
Leaders and Prophets Rebuked	Mic 3:1
Leaders commanded to help	1 Chr 22:17
Leadership of Moses	Acts 7:17
Leaven and salt	Lev 2:11
Leper cleansed	Mat 8:1
Leper cleansed	Mark 1:40
Leper cleansed	Luke 5:12
Leprosy in garments	Lev 13:47
Leprosy in houses	Lev 14:33
Let All Creation Praise God for Life	Psm 148:1 M
Let everything praise the LORD	Psm 150:1
Letter to Ar-ta-xerxes	Ezra 4:7
Letter to Shemaiah	Jer 29:24
Letter to the Exiles	Jer 29:1
Levi	1 Chr 6:1
Levite and His Concubine	Jud 19:1
Levites	Num 3:1
Levites	1 Chr 23:1
Levites not numbered	Num 1:47
Levites remain with Judah	2 Chr 11:18
Levites sanctify the temple	2 Chr 29:12
Levites separated from the people	Num 8:14
Levites' tithe of the tithe	Num 18:25
Levitical service appointed	2 Chr 31:2
Liberty threatened by legalism	Gal 5:1
Life by the Spirit	Gal 5:13
Life False Without God	Psm 36:1 M
Life God has assigned	1 Cor 7:17
Life in the Spirit	Rom 8:1
Life Through the Son	John 5:16
Life Through the Spirit	Rom 8:1
Life to the righteous	Hab 2:1
Linen Belt	Jer 13:1

List of Defeated Kings	Jos 12:1
List of the Exiles Who Returned	Ezra 2:1
List of the Exiles Who Returned	Neh 7:4
List of the Family Heads Returning With Ezra	Ezra 8:1
Listening and Doing	Jam 1:19
Litany of God's deliverance	Psm 136:10 R
Litany of God's wonders	Psm 136:1 R
Little Children and Jesus	Mat 19:13
Little Children and Jesus	Mark 10:13
Little Children and Jesus	Luke 18:15
Living as Children of Light	Eph 4:17
Living Creatures and the Glory of the LORD	Eze 1:1
Living for God	1 Pet 4:1
Living God and dead gods	Jer 10:11
Living Sacrifices	Rom 12:1
Living Stone and a Chosen People	1 Pet 2:4
Living the LORD's way	Psm 119:33
Living to Please God	1 Ths 4:1
Location and size of gates	Eze 40:19b
Locusts, Fire and a Plumb Line	Amos 7:1
Logic of the resurrection	1 Cor 15:29
Longing for comfort	Psm 119:81 R
Longing for the sanctuary	Psm 84:1
Loosing of Satan	Rev 20:7
LORD a faithful God	Psm 138:1
LORD Abhors the Pride of Israel	Amos 6:8
LORD and His Anointed Are Supreme	Psm 2:1 M
LORD Appears to Elijah	1 Kng 19:9
LORD appears to Moses	Deu 31:14
LORD Appears to Solomon	1 Kng 9:1
LORD Appears to Solomon	2 Chr 7:11
LORD Calls Samuel	1 Sam 3:1
LORD Cares for His Own	Psm 18:1 M
LORD Comes and Reigns	Zec 14:1
LORD Commands Joshua	Jos 1:1
LORD delivers the weak	Psm 35:1
LORD departs from the sanctuary	Eze 10:1
LORD God is a shepherd	Eze 34:11
LORD is God	Deu 4:32
LORD Is Judge	Psm 9:1 M

LORD known by His judgements	Eze 6:11
LORD my helper	Psm 30:1
Lord of the Sabbath	Mat 12:1
Lord of the Sabbath	Mark 2:23
Lord of the Sabbath	Luke 6:1
LORD of the thunderstorm	Psm 29:1
LORD our portion	Psm 119:57
LORD our refuge	Psm 11:1
LORD Promises to Bless Jerusalem	Zec 8:1
LORD provides and delivers	Psm 33:1
LORD Raises the Lowly	Psm 113:1 M
LORD raises up judges	Jud 2:16
LORD reigns in Zion	Mic 4:6
LORD Rejects Saul as King	1 Sam 15:1
LORD remembers his covenant	Psm 105:1
LORD restores Zion's fortunes	Psm 126:1
LORD Speaks	Job 38:1
LORD speaks out of the whirlwind	Job 38:1
LORD summons Moses to die	Deu 32:48
LORD the Deliver of His People	Psm 124:1 M
LORD the Homemaker for His People	Psm 127:1 M
LORD the House Keeper of His People	Psm 128:1 M
LORD the Object of His People's Praise	Psm 135:1 M
LORD the protector	Psm 125:1
LORD the Protector of His People	Psm 125:1 M
LORD the Restorer of His People	Psm 126:1 M
LORD the Satisfaction of His People	Psm 131:1 M
LORD the Trust of His People	Psm 132:1 M
LORD warns Solomon	1 Kng 11:9
LORD weighs the way of man	Pvb 16:1
LORD Will Appear	Zec 9:14
LORD Will Call for Judah	Zec 10:1
LORD will deliver His people	Isa 51:12
LORD Will Judge the Wicked	Psm 12:1 M
LORD will sustain	Psm 55:16
LORD's Anger Against Israel	Isa 9:8
LORD's Anger Against Israel	Hos 13:1
LORD's Anger Against Nineveh	Nah 1:2
LORD's Answer	Joel 2:18
LORD's Answer	Hab 1:5
LORD's Answer	Hab 2:2

LORD's blessing	Psm 118:21
LORD's blessings and love	Psm 107:33
LORD's Case Against Israel	Mic 6:1
LORD's covenant with Solomon	1 Kng 9:1
LORD's deeds of deliverance	Psm 135:8
LORD's deliverance	Psm 118:10
LORD's Devastation of the Earth	Isa 24:1
LORD's glory enters the temple	Eze 43:1
Lord's Grace to Paul	1 Tim 1:12
LORD's instructions to Joshua	Jos 1:1
LORD's Judgement on Ahaziah	2 Kng 1:1
LORD's love of Israel	Psm 149:1
LORD's mercy	Psm 118:1
LORD's mercy and vengeance	Deu 32:34
LORD's mighty right hand	Psm 118:15
LORD's Plan	Mic 4:6
LORD's promise to Joshua	Jos 3:7
LORD's promise to Solomon	2 Chr 7:11
Lord's Supper	Mat 26:14
Lord's Supper	Mark 14:12
Lord's Supper	1 Cor 11:17
LORD's sword drawn	Eze 21:1
LORD's wonderful works	Psm 111:1
LORD, Not Idols	Isa 44:6
Lord, the Rest of His People	Psm 134:1 M
Lot and His Daughters	Gen 19:30
Lot and his family flee	Gen 19:15
Lot chooses Sodom	Gen 13:8
Lot visited by two angels	Gen 19:1
Love	Rom 12:9
Love	1 Cor 12:31b
Love and faithfulness of God	Psm 57:1
Love and Obey the LORD	Deu 11:1
Love for Enemies	Mat 5:43
Love for Enemies	Luke 6:27
Love in action	1 John 3:11
Love of God and His People	Psm 45:1 M
Love of God's law	Psm 119:97
Love of Money	1 Tim 6:3
Love One Another	1 John 3:11
Love the LORD Your God	Deu 6:1

81

Love, for the Day Is Near	Rom 13:8
Loved One Dreams of Her Lover	Song 3:1 M
Lover	Song 1:8 N
Lover	Song 1:15 N
Lover	Song 1:17 N
Lover	Song 2:2 N
Lover	Song 2:14 N
Lover	Song 4:1 N
Lover	Song 5:1a N
Lover	Song 6:4 N
Lover	Song 6:13b N
Lover	Song 8:13 N
Lover Calls and Extols Her	Song 4:8 M
Lover Praises His Beloved	Song 6:4 M
Lover Praises His Beloved	Song 7:1 M
Lover Praises His Beloved	Song 7:6 M
Lover Sings His Loved One's Beauty	Song 4:1 M
Lover to His Beloved	Song 5:1a M
Lover to His Loved One	Song 1:9 M
Lover's Arrival	Song 3:6 M
Lust for money	Amos 8:4
Lydia's Conversion in Philippi	Acts 16:11
Lying prophet	1 Kng 13:11
Lying prophets	1 Kng 22:5
Lying Prophets	Jer 23:9

M

Macedonian call	Acts 16:6
Made Alive in Christ	Eph 2:1
Maiden	Song 6:11 M
Maiden and her family	Song 8:8
Maiden answers	Song 8:14
Maiden chooses the beloved	Song 4:16
Maiden contrasted to the court	Song 6:4
Maiden desires her beloved	Song 7:10
Maiden in the garden	Song 6:11
Maiden tells of her love	Song 5:10
Maiden thinks of her beloved	Song 1:12
Maiden to Her Distant Lover	Song 1:7 M
Maiden to Her Lover	Song 1:1 M

Maiden to the Daughters of Jerusalem	Song 1:5 M
Maiden's answer	Song 6:2
Maiden's Answer	Song 8:10 M
Maiden's beloved appears	Song 2:8
Maiden's Brothers	Song 8:8 M
Maiden's dream	Song 3:1
Maiden's reply	Song 6:13b
Majesty of the LORD	Psm 93:1
Majesty of the new Zion	Isa 60:15
Make the best of this life	Ecc 9:1
Making an altar of earth	Ex 20:21
Making of the veil	Ex 36:35
Making One's Calling and Election Sure	2 Pet 1:3
Man Among the Myrtle Trees	Zec 1:7
Man is born to trouble	Job 5:1
Man never satisfied	Pvb 27:17
Man of God From Judah	1 Kng 13:1
Man of God killed by a lion	1 Kng 13:20
Man of Lawlessness	2 Ths 2:1
Man placed in Eden	Gen 2:4
Man sent from the garden	Gen 3:20
Man who gives freely	Pvb 11:24
Man With a Measuring Line	Zec 2:1
Man With Leprosy	Mat 8:1
Man With Leprosy	Mark 1:40
Man With Leprosy	Luke 5:12
Man's limited knowledge	Job 38:16
Man's Plans and God's	Mic 2:1
Manasseh	1 Chr 7:14
Manasseh and Ephraim	Gen 48:1
Manasseh King of Judah	2 Kng 21:1
Manasseh King of Judah	2 Chr 33:1
Manasseh restores the altar	2 Chr 33:14
Manna and Quail	Ex 16:1
Manoah and the angel of the LORD	Jud 13:8
Manoah promised a child	Jud 13:2
Many Disciples Desert Jesus	John 6:60
Many Samaritans Believe	John 4:39
March, 1406 B.C.	Deu 31:1
March-April, 444 B.C.	Neh 2:1
March/April, 1445 B.C.	Num 9:1

March/April, 1446 B.C.	Ex 12:1
Marital joys and responsibilities	Pvb 5:15
Marks of a true apostle	2 Cor 12:11
Marriage	1 Cor 7:1
Marriage at the Resurrection	Mat 22:23
Marriage at the Resurrection	Mark 12:18
Marriage of heiresses	Num 36:1
Marriage supper of the Lamb	Rev 19:1
Marriage Violations	Deu 22:13
Married to Christ	Rom 7:1
Marrying a Captive Woman	Deu 21:10
Mary Visits Elizabeth	Luke 1:39
Mary's Song	Luke 1:46
Material splendor of Solomon	1 Kng 10:14
Materials for the Tabernacle	Ex 35:4
Materials Used	Ex 38:21
Matthew called	Mat 9:9
Matthew called	Mark 2:13
Matthias Chosen to Replace Judas	Acts 1:12
Meaning of the seventy weeks	Dan 9:20
Measurements of the temple area	Eze 42:15
Measuring line of Jerusalem	Zec 2:1
Medes execute judgement	Jer 51:11
Medium conjures up Samuel	1 Sam 28:15
Melchizedek blesses Abram	Gen 14:17
Melchizedek the Priest	Heb 7:1
Memories of a Returning Pilgrim	Psm 122:1 M
Men chosen to divide the land	Num 34:16
Men Fail Us; God Never	Psm 54:1 M
Menahem King of Israel	2 Kng 15:17
Mephibosheth's explanation	2 Sam 19:24
Merarites	Num 4:29
Merarites	1 Chr 23:21
Meriam becomes leprous	Num 12:9
Message About Ammon	Jer 49:1
Message About Babylon	Jer 50:1
Message About Damascus	Jer 49:23
Message About Edom	Jer 49:34
Message About Egypt	Jer 46:1
Message About Kedar and Hazor	Jer 49:28
Message About Moab	Jer 48:1

Message About the Philistines	Jer 47:1
Message of righteousness	Eze 33:10
Message to Baruch	Jer 45:1
Message to Ephesus	Rev 2:1
Message to Laodicea	Rev 3:14
Message to Pergamum	Rev 2:12
Message to Philadelphia	Rev 3:7
Message to Sardis	Rev 3:1
Message to Shemaiah	Jer 29:24
Message to Smyrna	Rev 2:8
Message to Thyatira	Rev 2:18
Messenger of the LORD to come	Isa 40:1
Messiah to restore Israel	Isa 11:10
Methuselah and Noah	Gen 5:25
Micah's Idols	Jud 17:1
Micah's idols and priest	Jud 17:1
Micah's idols and priest seized	Jud 18:14
Micaiah Prophesies Against Ahab	1 Kng 22:1
Micaiah Prophesies Against Ahab	2 Chr 18:1
Micaiah's true prophecy	1 Kng 22:13
Micaiah's true prophecy	2 Chr 18:12
Michal helps David escape	1 Sam 19:11
Michal rebukes David	2 Sam 6:20
Midianite raids on Israel	Jud 6:1
Might and grace of the LORD	Psm 147:1
Might deeds of God	Isa 63:10
Military and civil officials	1 Chr 27:1
Millennial reign	Rev 20:4
Ministers and keepers of the ark	1 Chr 16:37
Ministers of Baal Killed	2 Kng 10:18
Ministers of the New Covenant	2 Cor 2:12
Ministry of Paul	Col 1:24
Ministry of Reconciliation	2 Cor 5:11
Ministry of splendor	2 Cor 3:7 R
Miracle of water made into wine	John 2:1
Miriam and Aaron Oppose Moses	Num 12:1
Miscellaneous Laws	Deu 23:15
Miseries of the rich	Jam 5:1
Misery of the wicked	Job 18:5
Misery of the wicked	Psm 1:4
Missing silver cup	Gen 44:1

Mission of God's servant	Isa 42:1
Mission of the seventy	Luke 10:1
Mission of the twelve	Mark 6:7
Mission of the twelve	Luke 9:1
Moab Revolts	2 Kng 3:1
Moab Seduces Israel	Num 25:1
Moab's coming devastation	Isa 15:1
Moab's pride and fall	Isa 16:1
Molten sea and brass lavers	1 Kng 7:23
Monthly Offerings	Num 28:11
Moral Benefits of Wisdom	Pvb 2:1
Mordecai asks Esther for help	Est 4:4
Mordecai Honored	Est 6:1
Mordecai Persuades Esther to Help	Est 4:1
Mordecai Uncovers a Conspiracy	Est 2:19
More Proverbs of Solomon	Pvb 25:1
More Than Conquerors	Rom 8:28
Morning Prayer	Psm 5:1 M
Morning prayer	Psm 5:1 R
Mortal Body; an Immortal Spirit	Psm 49:1 M
Mortal man must perish	Job 4:12
Mortal Man's Eternal God	Psm 90:1 M
Moses and Aaron ask for release	Ex 10:1
Moses and the burning bush	Ex 3:1
Moses and the Glory of the LORD	Ex 33:12
Moses asks for meat	Num 11:10
Moses beholds God's glory	Ex 33:17
Moses Blesses the Tribes	Deu 33:1
Moses blesses the tribes of Israel	Deu 33:1
Moses commands obedience	Deu 4:1
Moses destroys the calf	Ex 32:15
Moses Flees to Midian	Ex 2:11
Moses forbidden to cross Jordan	Deu 3:23
Moses Forbidden to Cross the Jordan	Deu 3:21
Moses Inspects the Tabernacle	Ex 39:32
Moses intercedes for Israel	Deu 9:25
Moses meets God on Mount Sinai	Ex 19:16
Moses on the mountain	Ex 24:12
Moses pleads with God	Ex 32:11
Moses prays for the people	Num 16:15
Moses Returns to Egypt	Ex 4:18

Moses sets forth the law	Deu 4:44
Moses starts for Egypt	Ex 4:18
Moses tells of God's guidance	Deu 1:1
Moses to Die on Mount Nebo	Deu 32:48
Moses' birth	Ex 2:1
Moses' counsel to the Levites	Deu 31:24
Moses' crime and flight	Ex 2:11
Moses' shining face	Ex 34:29
Moses' Staff Becomes a Snake	Ex 7:6
Mother's Request	Mat 20:20
Mountain of the LORD	Isa 2:1
Mountain of the LORD	Mic 4:1
Mountain of the LORD to be blessed	Isa 25:6
Mourning for the One They Pierced	Zec 12:10
Multitudes healed	Mat 15:29
Murder	Mat 5:21
Murder of Amaziah	2 Chr 25:25
Murder of Ish-bosheth	2 Sam 4:1
Murder of the royal family	2 Chr 22:10
Murder reported to Israel	Jud 20:1
Murmuring of Israel	Deu 1:26
My times are in thy hand	Psm 31:14

N

Naaman Healed of Leprosy	2 Kng 5:1
Nabal's death	1 Sam 25:36
Naboth's Vineyard	1 Kng 21:1
Nadab King of Israel	1 Kng 15:25
Nahor's Sons	Gen 22:20
Names and mission of the twelve	Mat 10:1
Naomi and Ruth	Ruth 1:1
Naomi's land is sold	Ruth 4:1
Naphtali	1 Chr 7:13
Narrow and Wide Gates	Mat 7:13
Narrow Door	Luke 13:22
Nathan Rebukes David	2 Sam 12:1
Nathan's parable	2 Sam 12:1
Nathan's prophecy	2 Sam 7:1
Nathan's warning to David	1 Chr 17:1
Nation chosen as a witness	Isa 43:8

Nation's last days	Lam 4:17
Nation's sin and punishment	Isa 42:18
Nations conspire against the LORD	Psm 2:1
Nations invited to be saved	Isa 45:20
Nations Judged	Joel 3:1
Nations left to test Israel	Jud 3:1
Nations to seek God in Jerusalem	Zec 8:18
Nature of the resurrection	1 Cor 15:35
Nature's praise of the LORD	Psm 148:1
Nave and walls of the temple	Eze 41:1
Nazirite	Num 6:1
Near 621 B.C.	Jer 17:19
Nearness of Egypt's doom	Eze 30:1
Nebuchadnezzar glorifies God	Dan 3:26
Nebuchadnezzar to destroy Egypt	Jer 43:8
Nebuchadnezzar's Dream	Dan 2:1
Nebuchadnezzar's Dream of a Tree	Dan 4:1
Nebuchadnezzar's forgotten dream	Dan 2:1
Nebuchadnezzar's victory prophesied	Jer 27:1
Necessity of a preacher	Rom 10:14
Necessity of the resurrection	1 Cor 15:12
Need for workers	Mat 9:35
Need to interpret tongues	1 Cor 14:13
Nehemiah determined to rebuild	Neh 2:17
Nehemiah Helps the Poor	Neh 5:1
Nehemiah Inspects Jerusalem's Walls	Neh 2:11
Nehemiah's Final Reforms	Neh 13:1
Nehemiah's frugal diet	Neh 5:14
Nehemiah's inspection of the walls	Neh 2:9
Nehemiah's Prayer	Neh 1:1
Nehemiah's prayer for Israel	Neh 1:1
Neighbor and the enemy	Pvb 25:15
Neighbors and enemies	Mat 5:43
New Commandment	John 13:31
New covenant	Jer 31:31
New heaven and the new earth	Rev 21:1
New Heavens and a New Earth	Isa 65:17
New Jerusalem	Rev 21:1
New Jerusalem	Rev 21:9
New life with Christ	Eph 2:1
New Residents of Jerusalem	Neh 11:1

New Stone Tablets	Ex 34:1
New Temple Area	Eze 40:1
New temple arrangements	Eze 40:1
News of Saul's death	2 Sam 1:1
Nicodemus visits Jesus	John 3:1
Night at Gibe-ah	Jud 19:10
Nineveh to Fall	Nah 2:1
No Confidence in the Flesh	Plip 3:1
No Hope but God, Who Suffices	Psm 57:1 M
No One Is Righteous	Rom 3:9
No one is righteous before God	Job 25:1
No Other Gospel	Gal 1:6
Noise of destruction	Jer 51:54
North Gate	Eze 40:20
Northern Kings Defeated	Jos 11:1
Not Because of Israel's Righteousness	Deu 9:1
Not Circumcision but a New Creation	Gal 6:11
Not One Is Upright	Jer 5:1
Not Peace but Division	Luke 12:49
Number of David's armed men	1 Chr 12:23
Numbering of first-born sons	Num 3:40
Numbering of the Levite Clans	Num 4:34
Numbering of the Levites	Num 26:57
Numbering of the tribes	Num 26:5
Numbers and duties of the Levites	Num 3:5
Numerical proverbs	Pvb 30:15

O

Oath to put away foreign women	Ezra 10:1
Oaths	Mat 5:33
Oaths and retaliation	Mat 5:33
Obed is born: the Davidic line	Ruth 4:13
Obedience Commanded	Deu 4:1
Obedience in action	1 John 3:1
Obedience of Moses	Ex 40:16
Obedience to authority	Ecc 8:1
Obedient response of the servant	Isa 50:4
Obey the King	Ecc 8:2
Obligations of Christians	Plip 2:12
Observance of the Passover	2 Kng 23:21

Observance of the Passover	2 Chr 30:13
Observance of the Passover	2 Chr 35:10
Observance of the Sabbath	Ex 31:12
Observing the Passover at Gilgal	Jos 5:10
October, 444 B.C.	Neh 8:1
Offer of Life or Death	Deu 30:11
Offering and feast	1 Kng 8:62
Offering at the new moon	Num 28:11
Offering for sins done in ignorance	Num 15:22
Offering for the people	Lev 9:15
Offering for the priests	Lev 9:1
Offering for the saints	2 Cor 9:1
Offering for the tabernacle	Ex 25:1
Offering for the tabernacle	Ex 30:11
Offering for the tabernacle	Ex 35:20
Offering on the Sabbath	Num 28:9
Offering the first fruits	Deu 26:1
Offering the firstlings	Deu 15:19
Offerings and Holy Days	Eze 45:13
Offerings and music	1 Chr 16:1
Offerings at the Dedication of the Tabernacle	Num 7:1
Offerings brought for the Levites	2 Chr 31:11
Offerings for Priests and Levites	Num 18:8
Offerings for Priests and Levites	Deu 18:1
Offerings for Unintentional Sins	Num 15:22
Offerings of Abidan and Ahiezer	Num 7:60
Offerings of Cain and Abel	Gen 4:1
Offerings of Eliab and Elizur	Num 7:24
Offerings of Elishama and Gamaliel	Num 7:48
Offerings of Nahshon and Nethanel	Num 7:12
Offerings of Pagiel and Ahira	Num 7:72
Offerings of Shelumiel and Eliasaph	Num 7:36
Offerings of the prince	Eze 46:1
Offerings required of Israel	Num 15:1
Office of bishop	1 Tim 3:1
Office of Deacon	1 Tim 3:8
Officers and judges	1 Chr 26:29
Officers of the Tribes	1 Chr 27:16
Officers' and captains' offerings	Num 31:48
Officials to assist Solomon	1 Chr 28:1

Oil and Bread Set Before the LORD	Lev 24:1
Oil and the shewbread	Lev 24:1
Oil for the lamp	Ex 27:20
Oil for the Lampstand	Ex 27:20
Old life and the new	Eph 4:17
Omri King of Israel	1 Kng 16:21
On Cyprus	Acts 13:4
On Divisions in the Church	1 Cor 3:1
On the Road to Emmaus	Luke 24:13
On to Jerusalem	Acts 21:1
One Body, Many Parts	1 Cor 12:12
One in Christ	Eph 2:11
One Like a Son of Man	Rev 1:9
One Nation Under One King	Eze 38:1
One Place of Worship	Deu 12:1
Only Savior from Destructive Foes	Psm 142:1 M
Opposition to the Rebuilding	Ezra 4:1
Opposition to the Rebuilding	Neh 4:1
Oppression and desolation predicted	Amos 6:9
Oppression, Toil, Friendlessness	Ecc 4:1
Oppressors doomed to captivity	Isa 10:1
Oracle about the doom of Babylon	Isa 13:1
Oracles about Dumah and Arabia	Isa 21:11
Order to keep the commandments	Deu 11:8
Orderly Worship	1 Cor 14:26
Ordination of Aaron and His Sons	Lev 8:1
Ordination offering for priests	Lev 8:22
Other Clans of Judah	1 Chr 4:1
Other Priestly Garments	Ex 28:31
Other Priestly Garments	Ex 39:22
Other temple furnishings	1 Kng 7:40
Others Join David at Hebron	1 Chr 12:23
Others to settle west of Jordan	Num 32:16
Othniel	Jud 3:7
Othniel delivers Israel	Jud 3:7
Our Everlasting Redeemer	Psm 118:1 M
Our Faithful God	Psm 92:1 M
Our God Victorious	Psm 68:1 M
Our Heavenly Dwelling	2 Cor 5:1
Our Sovereign LORD	Psm 47:1 M
Outer Court	Eze 40:17

Overcome by trouble	Psm 55:1
Overseers and Deacons	1 Tim 3:1
Overthrow of Assyria	Isa 14:24

P

Palace buildings	1 Kng 7:1
Parable of potter and clay	Jer 18:1
Parable of the broken flask	Jer 19:1
Parable of the farmer	Isa 28:23
Parable of the fig tree	Luke 13:6
Parable of the Good Samaritan	Luke 10:25
Parable of the Great Banquet	Luke 14:15
Parable of the Growing Seed	Mark 4:26
Parable of the jars	Jer 13:12
Parable of the lighted lamp	Luke 11:33
Parable of the Lost Coin	Luke 15:8
Parable of the Lost Sheep	Mat 18:10
Parable of the Lost Sheep	Luke 15:1
Parable of the lost sheep	Luke 15:3
Parable of the Lost Son	Luke 15:11
Parable of the marriage feast	Luke 14:7
Parable of the Mustard Seed	Mark 4:30
Parable of the Net	Mat 13:47
Parable of the Persistent Widow	Luke 18:1
Parable of the Pharisee and the Tax Collector	Luke 18:9
Parable of the pounds	Luke 19:11
Parable of the Rich Fool	Luke 12:13
Parable of the salt	Luke 14:34
Parable of the Shrewd Manager	Luke 16:1
Parable of the Sower	Mat 13:1
Parable of the Sower	Mark 4:1
Parable of the Sower	Luke 8:1
Parable of the sower	Luke 8:4
Parable of the sower explained	Mat 13:18
Parable of the sower explained	Mark 4:10
Parable of the sower explained	Luke 8:9
Parable of the Talents	Mat 25:14
Parable of the ten maidens	Mat 25:1
Parable of the Ten Minas	Luke 19:11

Parable of the Ten Virgins	Mat 25:1
Parable of the Tenants	Mat 21:33
Parable of the Tenants	Mark 12:1
Parable of the Tenants	Luke 20:9
Parable of the Two Sons	Mat 21:28
Parable of the unforgiving servant	Mat 18:23
Parable of the Unmerciful Servant	Mat 18:21
Parable of the unrighteous steward	Luke 16:1
Parable of the vine	Eze 15:1
Parable of the vineyard	Isa 5:1
Parable of the waistcloth	Jer 13:1
Parable of the watching servants	Luke 12:35
Parable of the Wedding Banquet	Mat 22:1
Parable of the Weeds	Mat 13:24
Parable of the Weeds Explained	Mat 13:36
Parable of the wicked tenants	Mat 21:33
Parable of the wicked tenants	Mark 12:1
Parable of the wicked tenants	Luke 20:9
Parable of the widow and the judge	Luke 18:1
Parable of the worker in the vineyard	Mat 20:1
Parable of the Workers in the Vineyard	Mat 20:1
Parables about the kingdom	Mat 13:24
Parables about the kingdom	Mark 4:21
Parables about the kingdom	Luke 13:18
Parables of the Hidden Treasure and the Pearl	Mat 13:44
Parables of the Mustard Seed and the Yeast	Mat 13:31
Parables of the Mustard Seed and the Yeast	Luke 13:18
Parables of the tower and the king	Luke 14:25
Paralytic healed and forgiven	Mat 9:1 R
Paralytic healed and forgiven	Mark 2:1 R
Paralytic healed and forgiven	Luke 5:17 R
Passover	Ex 12:1
Passover	Num 9:1
Passover	Num 28:16
Passover	Deu 16:1
Passover	Ezra 6:19
Passover and unleavened bread	Lev 23:4
Passover command	Num 9:1
Passover Restrictions	Ex 12:43
Pastor as an example	1 Tim 4:11

Pastoral duties to elders	1 Tim 5:17
Pastoral duties to slaves	1 Tim 6:1
Pastoral duties to widows	1 Tim 5:3
Patience in Suffering	Jam 5:7
Patience of the saints	Jam 5:7
Paul Accepted by the Apostles	Gal 2:1
Paul accepted by the church	Gal 2:1
Paul and Barnabas on Cyprus	Acts 13:1
Paul and Barnabas return to Antioch	Acts 14:19
Paul and Silas imprisoned	Acts 16:16
Paul and Silas in Prison	Acts 16:16
Paul and the False Apostles	2 Cor 11:1
Paul Arrested	Acts 21:27
Paul at Athens	Acts 17:16
Paul at Beroea	Acts 17:10
Paul at Corinth	Acts 18:1
Paul at Thessalonica	Acts 17:1
Paul baptizes John's disciples	Acts 19:1
Paul Before Agrippa	Acts 25:23
Paul Boasts About His Sufferings	2 Cor 11:16
Paul Called by God	Gal 1:11
Paul describes his conversion	Acts 26:12
Paul escapes to Jerusalem	Acts 9:23
Paul in Ephesus	Acts 19:1
Paul in Jerusalem	Acts 21:15
Paul Opposes Peter	Gal 2:11
Paul preaches at Damascus	Acts 9:19b
Paul Preaches at Rome Under Guard	Acts 28:17
Paul returns to Antioch	Acts 18:18
Paul Sails to Rome	Acts 27:1
Paul sent to Rome	Acts 27:1
Paul Speaks to the Crowd	Acts 21:37
Paul speaks to the Ephesian elders	Acts 20:17
Paul stays within God's limits	2 Cor 10:13
Paul taken to Caesarea	Acts 23:23
Paul the Minister to the Gentiles	Rom 15:14
Paul the Preacher to the Gentiles	Eph 3:1
Paul the Roman Citizen	Acts 22:22
Paul Transferred to Caesarea	Acts 23:23
Paul travels to Caesarea	Acts 21:1
Paul tried before Agrippa	Acts 26:1

Paul tried before Felix	Acts 24:1
Paul tried before Festus	Acts 25:1
Paul visits Macedonia and Achaia	Acts 20:1
Paul's appeal to Agrippa	Acts 26:24
Paul's arrest	Acts 21:27
Paul's Arrival at Jerusalem	Acts 21:17
Paul's authority of divine origin	Gal 1:11
Paul's boldness in prison	Plip 1:12
Paul's case discussed	Acts 25:13
Paul's Chains Advance the Gospel	Plip 1:12
Paul's Change of Plans	2 Cor 1:12
Paul's Charge to Timothy	1 Tim 6:11
Paul's Charge to Timothy	2 Tim 3:10
Paul's Concern for the Corinthians	2 Cor 12:11
Paul's Concern for the Galatians	Gal 4:8
Paul's concern for the Galatians	Gal 4:12
Paul's defense	Acts 21:37
Paul's Defense of His Ministry	2 Cor 10:1
Paul's Farewell to the Ephesian Elders	Acts 20:13
Paul's fear of false teachers	2 Cor 11:1
Paul's future plans	Rom 15:22
Paul's Hardships	2 Cor 6:3
Paul's itinerary	1 Cor 16:5
Paul's Joy	2 Cor 7:2
Paul's Labor for the Church	Col 1:24
Paul's Longing to See the Thessalonians	1 Ths 2:17
Paul's Longing to Visit Rome	Rom 1:8
Paul's Ministry in Thessalonica	1 Ths 2:1
Paul's opposition to Cephas (*Peter*)	Gal 2:11
Paul's Personal benediction	Gal 6:11
Paul's Plan to Visit Rome	Rom 15:23
Paul's Plea for Onesimus	Plem 8
Paul's prayer for the Colossians	Col 1:9
Paul's reason for writing	Rom 15:14
Paul's reception in Thessalonica	1 Ths 2:13
Paul's reply to charges against him	2 Cor 10:1
Paul's rightful boasting	2 Cor 11:16
Paul's sorrow for Israel	Rom 9:1
Paul's trial before the Sanhedrin	Acts 22:30
Paul's Vision and His Thorn	2 Cor 12:1
Paul's Vision of the Man of Macedonia	Acts 16:6

Paul's visions of the Lord	2 Cor 12:1
Paul's work in Ephesus	Acts 19:8
Paul's work in Thessalonica	1 Ths 2:1
Paul, apostle to the Gentiles	Eph 3:1
Paying Taxes to Caesar	Mat 22:15
Paying Taxes to Caesar	Mark 12:13
Paying Taxes to Caesar	Luke 20:20
Peace and Joy	Rom 5:1
Peace in keeping God's law	Psm 119:161
Peace of Jerusalem	Psm 122:1
Pekah King of Israel	2 Kng 15:27
Pekahiah King of Israel	2 Kng 15:23
Penalty for not cleansing	Num 19:20
Penitent thief	Luke 23:39
Penitential Cry for Help	Psm 143:1 M
Penitent's prayer	Psm 51:1
Pentecost and feast of trumpets	Lev 23:15
People and princes condemned	Eze 22:23
People Complain	Num 11:1
People flee	Jer 51:45
People in Jerusalem	1 Chr 9:1
People living in Jerusalem	Neh 11:3
People Rebel	Num 14:1
People returning with Ezra	Ezra 8:1
People returning with Zerubbabel	Ezra 2:1
People's Confession of Sin	Ezra 10:1
Perez and Zerah born	Gen 38:24
Persecuted Turns to God	Psm 59:1 M
Persecution of the church	Acts 8:1b
Personal Greetings	Rom 16:1
Personal Injuries	Ex 21:12
Personal observations	Pvb 30:1
Personal Remarks	2 Tim 4:9
Personal Requests	1 Cor 16:5
Persons excluded from the assembly	Deu 23:1
Perversion of justice	Hab 1:2
Pestilence upon Israel	2 Sam 24:15
Peter Addresses the Crowd	Acts 2:14
Peter and John arrested	Acts 4:1
Peter and John Before the Sanhedrin	Acts 4:1
Peter and John set free	Acts 4:13

Peter at Cornelius' House	Acts 10:23b
Peter delivered from prison	Acts 12:6
Peter Disowns Jesus	Mat 26:69
Peter Disowns Jesus	Mark 14:66
Peter Disowns Jesus	Luke 22:54
Peter Explains His Actions	Acts 11:1
Peter heals Aeneas	Acts 9:32
Peter Heals the Crippled Beggar	Acts 3:1
Peter Speaks to the Onlookers	Acts 3:11
Peter's Confession of Christ	Mat 16:13
Peter's Confession of Christ	Luke 9:18
Peter's confession of faith	Mat 16:13
Peter's confession of faith	Mark 8:27
Peter's confession of faith	Luke 9:18
Peter's Defense	Acts 4:5
Peter's denial foretold	Mark 14:26
Peter's denial foretold	Luke 22:31
Peter's denial foretold	John 13:36
Peter's denial of Jesus	Mat 26:69
Peter's denial of Jesus	Mark 14:66
Peter's denial of Jesus	Luke 22:54
Peter's First Denial	John 18:15
Peter's great affirmation	John 6:66
Peter's Miraculous Escape From Prison	Acts 12:1
Peter's mother-in-law healed	Mat 8:14
Peter's mother-in-law healed	Mark 1:29
Peter's mother-in-law healed	Luke 4:38
Peter's Pentecostal sermon	Acts 2:14
Peter's Second and Third Denials	John 18:25
Peter's sermon in the temple area	Acts 3:11
Peter's sermon to Cornelius	Acts 10:34
Peter's Vision	Acts 10:9
Peter's visit to Cornelius	Acts 10:23b
Petition of One Betrayed	Psm 109:1 M
Petition to be saved from death	Psm 88:1 R
Pharaoh makes Joseph a ruler	Gen 41:37
Pharaoh pursues Israel	Ex 14:5
Pharaoh refuses to let Israel go	Ex 5:1
Pharaoh tells his dream to Joseph	Gen 41:14
Pharaoh's command to the midwives	Ex 1:15
Pharaoh's dream	Gen 41:1

Pharisee and the publican	Luke 18:9
Pharisees ask for a sign	Mat 16:1
Pharisees ask for a sign	Mark 8:11
Pharisees Investigate the Healing	John 9:13
Pharisees plot to kill Jesus	John 11:45
Pharisees question the healed man	John 9:13
Philip and Nathana-el follow Jesus	John 1:43
Philip and the Ethiopian	Acts 8:26
Philip at Samaria	Acts 8:4
Philip in Samaria	Acts 8:4
Philistines Capture the Ark	1 Sam 4:1
Philistines capture the ark	1 Sam 5:1
Philistines defeated	2 Sam 5:17
Philistines defeated at Mizpah	1 Sam 7:5
Philistines dismiss David	1 Sam 29:1
Philistines flee	1 Sam 14:16
Philistines Subdued at Mizpah	1 Sam 7:2
Piety and almsgiving	Mat 6:1
Pillars of cloud and fire	Ex 13:17
Place to worship God	Acts 7:44 R
Places yet to be captured	Jud 1:22
Plague and pestilence in Israel	Amos 4:9
Plague as a punishment	1 Chr 21:7
Plague averted	2 Sam 24:18
Plague of Boils	Ex 9:8
Plague of boils and sores	Ex 9:8
Plague of darkness	Ex 10:21
Plague of Flies	Ex 8:20
Plague of frogs	Ex 7:25
Plague of gnats	Ex 8:16
Plague of Hail	Ex 9:13
Plague of hail and fire	Ex 9:22
Plague of Locusts	Ex 10:1
Plague of locusts	Ex 10:12
Plague of locusts	Joel 1:2
Plague of locusts	Amos 7:1
Plague of locusts	Rev 9:1
Plague on Livestock	Ex 9:1
Plague on the Firstborn	Ex 11:1
Plague on the people	Num 16:41
Plagues upon men	Rev 16:1

Plan to defeat Ai	Jos 8:1
Plans to return the ark	1 Sam 6:1
Plea for renewal of the covenant	Psm 89:38
Plea for vindication	Psm 35:17 R
Plea for vindication	Psm 43:1 R
Pleasures Are Meaningless	Ecc 2:1
Plight of the psalmist	Psm 69:1
Plot Against Jeremiah	Jer 11:18
Plot Against Jesus	Mat 26:1
Plot against the Jews	Dan 3:8
Plot to kill Ahasu-erus fails	Est 2:19
Plot to kill Jeremiah	Jer 18:18
Plot to kill Jesus	Mat 26:1
Plot to kill Jesus	Mark 14:1
Plot to kill Jesus	Luke 22:1
Plot to Kill Jesus	John 11:45
Plot to kill Joseph	Gen 37:12
Plot to Kill Paul	Acts 23:12
Plotting of Sanballat and Tobiah	Neh 4:1
Plunder of the land	Dan 11:20
Plundering the Syrian camp	2 Kng 7:16
Poisonous food made harmless	2 Kng 4:38
Portion for priests	Lev 7:28
Portion for the priests	Deu 18:1
Position of women	1 Tim 2:8
Positive instructions to a son	Pvb 4:20
Possessing the land of Canaan	Num 33:50
Possessions and masters	Mat 6:19
Postscript	Hos 14:9
Power and dominion of the LORD	Psm 97:1
Power and might of Mordecai	Est 10:1
Power of faith	Mark 11:20
Power of the Leviathan	Job 41:1
Power of the northern king	Dan 11:36
Practical appeals	1 Ths 5:12
Praise and Obedience to God	Psm 95:1 M
Praise and Prayer	Isa 63:7
Praise for Deliverance	Psm 21:1 M
Praise for God's steadfast love	Psm 117:1
Praise for the LORD's goodness	Psm 92:1
Praise the work of God	Job 36:24

Praise to a faithful, mighty God	Psm 89:5
Praise to a holy God	Psm 99:1
Praise to a righteous LORD	Psm 98:1
Praise to God All-Bountiful	Psm 145:1 M
Praise to God for a Living Hope	1 Pet 1:3
Praise to God for deliverance	Psm 9:1
Praise to the LORD	Psm 135:1
Praise to the LORD	Isa 25:1
Praise to the LORD for His Gracious Deliverance	Psm 138:1 M
Prayer	Mat 6:5
Prayer and confession	Jam 5:13
Prayer and deliverance of Jonah	Jon 2:1
Prayer and fasting	Mat 6:5
Prayer and Praise	Mic 7:14
Prayer and the Golden Rule	Mat 7:7
Prayer Because of a False Friend	Psm 55:1 M
Prayer during distress	Psm 32:1 R
Prayer for Continued Mercies	Psm 85:1 M
Prayer for Deliverance	Psm 7:1 M
Prayer for Deliverance	Psm 13:1 M
Prayer for deliverance	Psm 54:1 R
Prayer for deliverance	Psm 69:13
Prayer for deliverance	Psm 86:1
Prayer for deliverance	Psm 120:1 R
Prayer for Deliverance from Sin and Sinners	Psm 141:1 M
Prayer for Divine Aid in Distress	Psm 123:1 M
Prayer for God's Fatherly Protection	Psm 69:1 M
Prayer for God's favor	Psm 90:13 R
Prayer for God's Help	Psm 74:1 M
Prayer for grace to keep God's law	Psm 119:129
Prayer for guidance and protection	Psm 25:1
Prayer for help	Psm 28:1 R
Prayer for Help Against the Ungodly	Psm 83:1 M
Prayer for holiness	1 Ths 3:11 R
Prayer for Judgement on the Wicked	Psm 10:1 M
Prayer for Mercy	Psm 6:1 M
Prayer for mercy during trouble	Psm 6:1
Prayer for mercy to Israel	Psm 85:1
Prayer for national deliverance	Psm 60:1 R

Prayer for Protection	Psm 17:1 M
Prayer for Retribution on Jerusalem's Destroyers	Psm 79:1 M
Prayer for Righteous Ruling By Solomon	Psm 72:1 M
Prayer for Safety from Enemies	Psm 35:1 M
Prayer for Salvation	Psm 80:1 M
Prayer for Salvation and Forgiveness	Psm 25:1 M
Prayer for Silent Assurance	Psm 39:1 M
Prayer for Speedy Aid	Psm 70:1 M
Prayer for the church	John 17:20
Prayer for the disciples	John 17:6
Prayer for the Ephesians	Eph 3:14
Prayer for the king	Psm 20:1 R
Prayer for the king	Psm 72:1 R
Prayer for understanding	Psm 119:169 R
Prayer for understanding the law	Psm 119:25
Prayer for Victory	Psm 20:1 M
Prayer for Victory	Psm 60:1 M
Prayer for wisdom and knowledge	Eph 1:15
Prayer for wisdom granted	1 Kng 3:3
Prayer in Severe Illness	Psm 88:1 M
Prayer of a believing heart	Psm 139:1
Prayer of a soul in distress	Psm 143:1
Prayer of a wronged man	Psm 7:1
Prayer of an aged man	Psm 71:1
Prayer of an Aged Worshiper	Psm 71:1 M
Prayer of Confession	Psm 51:1 M
Prayer of Faith	Jam 5:13
Prayer of mercy	Lam 5:19 R
Prayer of thankfulness	Plip 1:3
Prayer of the troubled heart	Psm 61:1
Prayer to be glorified	John 17:1
Prayer to defeat Israel's enemies	Psm 83:1
Preaching at Iconium	Acts 14:1
Preaching at Lystra	Acts 14:8
Preaching in Perga and Antioch	Acts 13:13
Preaching of John the Baptist	Mat 3:1
Preaching of John the Baptist	Mark 1:4
Preaching of John the Baptist	Luke 3:1
Preface to the Book of Acts	Acts 1:1
Preface to the Book of Luke	Luke 1:1

Prelude to the seven seals	Rev 5:1
Preparation for the Passover	2 Chr 35:1
Preparation for the return	Ezra 1:5
Preparation to return to Jerusalem	Ezra 8:21
Preparations for Building the Temple	1 Kng 5:1
Preparations for Building the Temple	2 Chr 2:1
Preparations for crossing the Jordan	Jos 1:10
Preparations for the Temple	1 Chr 22:2
Preparing to build the temple	1 Kng 5:1
Preparing to build the temple	1 Chr 22:1
Preparing to build the temple	2 Chr 2:1
Preparing to move the ark	1 Chr 15:1
Presence of God in calamity	Psm 46:1
Pressing on Toward the Goal	Plip 3:12
Price of Wisdom	Pvb 17:13
Pride and shame of Jerusalem	Jer 13:15
Pride of Moab	Jer 48:28
Priest and Levites who returned	Neh 7:39
Priest's breastpiece	Ex 28:15
Priest's breastpiece	Ex 39:8
Priest's portion	Num 18:8
Priest's robe	Ex 28:31
Priestly Blessing	Num 6:22
Priestly Garments	Ex 28:1
Priestly Garments	Ex 39:1
Priests and Levites	Neh 12:1
Priests and Levites assembled	1 Chr 23:1
Priests and the holy things	Lev 22:1
Priests Begin Their Ministry	Lev 9:1
Priests married to foreign women	Ezra 10:18
Priests of Baal on Mount Carmel	1 Kng 18:20
Priests' chambers	Eze 42:1
Priests' Share	Lev 7:28
Prince and inheritance laws	Eze 46:16
Prince, the Levites, the Priests	Eze 44:1
Prior to 605 B.C.	Jer 18:1
Prior to 605 B.C.	Jer 48:1
Priority of Melchizedek priesthood	Heb 7:1
Priscilla, Aquila and Apollos	Acts 18:18
Prisoner's prayer	Psm 142:1
Privileges of living in Zion	Psm 87:1

Problem of unsound doctrine	1 Tim 1:3
Proclamation of Cyrus	Ezra 1:1
Proclamation of the Passover	2 Chr 30:1
Prohibition of idol feasts	1 Cor 10:14
Prologue	Job 1:1
Prologue	Rev 1:1
Prologue: Purpose and Theme	Pvb 1:1
Promise of a land	Gen 15:17
Promise of a prophet	Deu 18:15
Promise of Christ's coming	2 Pet 3:1
Promise of deliverance	Isa 37:21
Promise of destruction	Isa 42:14
Promise of Egypt's destruction	Eze 30:20
Promise of exile and return	Jer 27:12
Promise of God's protection	Ex 23:20
Promise of God's wrath	Eze 22:17
Promise of greater works	John 14:12
Promise of peace	John 14:25
Promise of rest	Heb 4:1
Promise of Restoration	Jer 33:1
Promise of restoration	Eze 16:53
Promise of return from exile	Jer 16:14
Promise of the redeemed	Psm 107:1
Promise of the Spirit	John 14:15
Promise to David and Zion	Psm 132:11
Promise to Sarai	Gen 17:15
Promised Glory of the New House	Hag 2:1
Promised outpouring of the spirit	Joel 2:28
Promised Return of Israel	Eze 11:16
Promised Ruler From Bethlehem	Mic 5:1
Promotion of Haman	Est 3:1
Promotion of Mordecai	Est 8:1
Pronouncement of a curse	Psm 69:22
Prophecies against Ammon and Moab	Eze 25:1
Prophecies against Edom and Ammon	Amos 1:11
Prophecies against Gaza and Tyre	Amos 1:6
Prophecies against Moab and Judah	Amos 2:1
Prophecy About Egypt	Isa 19:1
Prophecy about Egypt	Jer 46:2
Prophecy about Israel	Jer 46:25
Prophecy About Jerusalem	Isa 22:1

Prophecy about Josiah	1 Kng 13:1
Prophecy about Nebuchadnezzar	Jer 46:13
Prophecy About Tyre	Isa 23:1
Prophecy against Ammon	Jer 49:1
Prophecy Against Ammon	Eze 25:1
Prophecy Against Assyria	Isa 14:24
Prophecy Against Babylon	Isa 13:1
Prophecy Against Babylon	Isa 21:1
Prophecy against Babylon	Jer 50:1
Prophecy Against Cush	Isa 18:1
Prophecy against Damascus	Amos 1:3
Prophecy against Edom	Jer 49:7
Prophecy Against Edom	Eze 25:12
Prophecy Against Edom	Eze 35:1
Prophecy against Elam	Jer 49:34
Prophecy Against Egypt	Eze 29:1 R
Prophecy Against Egypt and Cush	Isa 20:1
Prophecy against false prophetesses	Eze 13:17
Prophecy against false prophets	Eze 13:1
Prophecy Against Gog	Eze 38:1
Prophecy against Israel	Amos 2:6
Prophecy against Israel's shepherds	Eze 34:1
Prophecy against Kedar	Jer 49:28
Prophecy Against Moab	Isa 15:1
Prophecy against Moab	Jer 48:1
Prophecy Against Moab	Eze 25:8
Prophecy against Mount Seir	Eze 35:1
Prophecy against Philistia	Jer 47:1
Prophecy Against Philistia	Eze 25:15
Prophecy Against Sidon	Eze 28:20
Prophecy Against the House of Eli	1 Sam 2:27
Prophecy Against the King of Tyre	Eze 28:1
Prophecy Against the Mountains of Israel	Eze 6:1
Prophecy Against the Philistines	Isa 14:28
Prophecy Against the South	Eze 20:45
Prophecy Against Tyre	Eze 26:1
Prophecy and tongues	1 Cor 14:1
Prophecy of doom to Eli	1 Sam 2:27
Prophecy of Elisha	2 Kng 6:32
Prophecy of restoration	Hos 1:10
Prophecy of Scripture	2 Pet 1:12

Prophecy to the Mountains of Israel	Eze 36:1
Prophet Azariah advises Asa	2 Chr 15:1
Prophet Condemns Ahab	1 Kng 20:35
Prophet not heeded	Eze 33:30
Prophet Without Honor	Mat 13:53
Prophet Without Honor	Mark 6:1
Prophet's call and commission	Jer 1:1
Prophets' false dreams	Jer 23:23
Prophets' false message	Jer 23:16
Propriety in Worship	1 Cor 11:2
Prosperity After Turning to the LORD	Deu 30:1
Prosperity of the righteous	Psm 112:1
Prosperity of the wicked	Job 21:1
Protection of Property	Ex 22:1
Proverbs of Solomon	Pvb 10:1
Provision for special offerings	Deu 12:15
Provision for teaching the law	Deu 31:9
Provision for the Levites	Jos 13:32
Psalm for the Thank Offering	Psm 100:1 M
Psalm of praise and trust	Psm 34:1 P
Psalm of Refuge	Psm 16:1 M
Psalm of the compassionate	Psm 41:1
Psalmist has kept God's law	Psm 119:121
Punishment by the Chaldeans	Hab 1:5
Punishment for idolatry	Deu 4:25
Punishment for Israel	Hos 9:1
Punishment for turning from God	Deu 29:16
Punishment in the fiery furnace	Dan 3:16
Punishment is at hand	Jer 2:29
Punishment of Babylon	Jer 51:1
Punishment of Oholibah	Eze 23:22
Punishment of the Gibeonites	Jos 9:16
Punishment of the prince of Israel	Eze 21:24
Punishment of the rebels	Num 16:25
Punishment of the wicked	Psm 58:1
Punishments for disobedience	Lev 26:14
Punishments for sin	Lev 20:1
Purification after childbirth	Lev 12:1
Purification of the Levites	Num 8:5
Purification of the unclean	Num 19:1
Purification of those who killed	Num 31:13

Purim Celebrated	Est 9:18
Purity of the Camp	Num 5:1
Purity the fruit of the law	Psm 119:9
Purpose of Proverbs	Pvb 1:1
Purpose of the law	Deu 6:1

Q

Quail From the LORD	Num 11:4
Quails and manna provided	Ex 16:13
Qualification for elders	Titus 1:5
Queen of Sheba Visits Solomon	1 Kng 10:1
Queen of Sheba Visits Solomon	2 Chr 9:1
Queen Vashti Deposed	Est 1:1
Question about David's son	Mat 22:41
Question about David's son	Mark 12:35
Question about David's son	Luke 20:41
Question about fasting	Mat 9:14
Question about fasting	Mark 2:18
Question about fasting	Luke 5:33
Questioning disciples	John 6:60

R

Rabshakeh urges peace with Assyria	2 Kng 18:28
Rachel steals the household gods	Gen 31:33
Radiant Face of Moses	Ex 34:29
Rahab and the Spies	Jos 2:1
Raising of the widow's son	Luke 7:11
Raven and dove sent	Gen 8:6
Reading of the Law	Deu 31:9
Reading of the law	2 Chr 34:29
Reading of the scroll	Jer 36:9
Reason for building the altar	Jos 22:21
Reason for parables	Mat 13:10
Rebekah at the well	Gen 24:15
Rebekah goes with the servant	Gen 24:50
Rebekah schemes with Jacob	Gen 27:5
Rebekah's scheme	Gen 27:41
Rebellion Against the LORD	Deu 1:26

Rebellion and death of Jehoiakim	2 Kng 24:1
Rebellion of God's people	Neh 9:26
Rebellion of Israel	Num 14:1
Rebellion of Korah	Num 16:1
Rebellious Israel	Eze 20:1
Rebellious Judah to be crushed	Isa 30:8
Rebellious Nation	Isa 1:2
Rebellious Son	Deu 21:18
Rebuilding begun	Neh 3:1
Rebuilding of the temple begun	Ezra 3:8
Rebuilding the Altar	Ezra 3:1
Rebuilding the Temple	Ezra 3:7
Reburial of Saul and Jonathan	2 Sam 21:10
Recabites	Jer 35:1
Receiving the Spirit by faith	Gal 3:1
Reconciling ministry	2 Cor 5:11 R
Recovery of the house of Israel	Eze 28:24
Recovery of the lost axe head	2 Kng 6:1
Redeemer to restore His people	Isa 43:14
Redeeming the tithe	Lev 27:30
Redeeming What Is the LORD's	Lev 27:1
Redemption of God's people	Zec 10:1
Redemption of property	Lev 25:25
Redemption of servants	Lev 25:39
Redemption or destruction	Isa 1:18
Reforms by Jehoshaphat	2 Chr 19:1
Reforms of Josiah	2 Kng 23:4
Refugees rebuked	Jer 44:1
Refugees to perish in Egypt	Jer 44:11
Refusal to heed the prophets	Jer 7:21
Refusal to repent	Jer 6:16
Regathering of Israel	Eze 39:25
Regulations About Infectious Skin Diseases	Lev 13:1
Regulations About Mildew	Lev 13:47
Regulations and rituals condemned	Col 2:16
Rehoboam erects fortresses	2 Chr 11:1
Rehoboam Fortifies Judah	2 Chr 11:5
Rehoboam King of Judah	1 Kng 14:21
Rehoboam's Family	2 Chr 11:18
Rehoboam's harsh rule	2 Chr 10:1
Rehoboam, king of Israel	1 Kng 12:1

Rehoboam, king of Judah	1 Kng 14:21
Reign of the king	Zec 9:11
Reign of the LORD	Isa 24:17
Reign of the righteous	Pvb 29:1
Rejection of the king	Zec 11:1
Rejoicing in the LORD	Hab 3:16
Relation of Israel to God	Amos 3:1
Remember the tables of stone	Deu 9:6
Remember Your Creator While Young	Ecc 11:7
Remnant and the true king	Jer 23:1
Remnant of Israel	Isa 10:20
Remnant of Israel	Rom 11:1
Remnant of Israel to be saved	Isa 10:20 R
Remnant to be preserved	Eze 6:8 R
Removal of Queen Vashti	Est 1:10
Rend Your Heart	Joel 2:12
Render Praise to God's Majesty	Psm 96:1 M
Renewal of the covenant	Ex 33:1
Renewal of the Covenant	Deu 29:1
Renewal of the covenant	2 Kng 23:1
Repent or Perish	Luke 13:1
Repentance and restoration	Hos 5:15
Repentance to Bring Blessing	Hos 14:1
Repeopling of Jerusalem	Neh 11:1
Reply	Song 1:8 M
Report of immorality	1 Cor 5:1 R
Report of the Danite spies	Jud 18:1
Report of the spies	Deu 1:19
Report on the Exploration	Num 13:26
Report to the believers	Acts 4:23
Reproof for Diotrephes	3 John 9
Request for Prayer	2 Ths 3:1
Request for prayer	Heb 13:18
Request of James and John	Mark 10:35
Requirements of the priests	Lev 10:8
Rescue of Rahab	Jos 6:22
Responsibilities of marriage	1 Cor 7:10
Rest for the Weary	Mat 11:25
Rest of the Levites	1 Chr 24:20
Restoration of Ephraim	Jer 31:15
Restoration of Israel	Isa 49:8

Restoration of Israel	Jer 30:1
Restoration of Jerusalem	Jer 33:1
Restoration of Judah	Jer 31:23
Restoration of kings and priests	Jer 33:14
Restoration of the temple	2 Chr 24:8
Restoration of Zion	Isa 62:1
Result of the drought	Joel 1:11
Results of justification by faith	Rom 5:1
Results of the census	Num 4:34
Resurrection	Mat 28:1
Resurrection	Mark 16:1
Resurrection	Luke 24:1
Resurrection Body	1 Cor 15:35
Resurrection of Christ	1 Cor 15:1
Resurrection of Jesus	Mat 28:1
Resurrection of Jesus	Mark 16:1
Resurrection of Jesus	Luke 24:1
Resurrection of Jesus	John 20:1
Resurrection of the Dead	1 Cor 15:12
Return of the seventy	Luke 10:17
Return of the spies	Jos 2:22
Return of the unclean spirits	Mat 12:43
Return to Antioch in Syria	Acts 14:21
Return to dry land	Gen 8:13
Return to Jerusalem	Ezra 8:15
Return to Nazareth	Mat 2:19
Return to Zion promised	Isa 35:1
Reuben	1 Chr 5:1
Reuben and Gad settle in Gilead	Num 32:1
Revenge for Dinah	Gen 34:18
Revenge of Samson	Jud 15:1
Revere God's Authority and His Holiness	Psm 99:1 M
Revolt led by Jehoiada	2 Chr 23:1
Revolt of the ten tribes	1 Kng 12:12
Revolt of the ten tribes	2 Chr 10:12
Reward for Obedience	Lev 26:1
Reward of a cheerful heart	Pvb 15:13
Reward of the righteous	Psm 18:20
Reward of the righteous	Mat 10:34
Reward of the wicked	Job 27:13
Reward of wisdom	Pvb 2:1

Rewards of repentance	Deu 30:1
Rewriting of the scroll	Jer 36:27
Rich and the poor	Pvb 14:20
Rich Man and Lazarus	Luke 16:19
Rich Ruler	Luke 18:18
Rich Young Man	Mat 19:16
Rich Young Man	Mark 10:17
Rich young ruler	Mat 19:16
Rich young ruler	Mark 10:17
Rich young ruler	Luke 18:18
Riches and splendor of Ahasu-erus	Est 1:1
Riches Are Meaningless	Ecc 5:8
Rider on the White Horse	Rev 19:11
Right and wrong fasting	Isa 58:1
Right of the Firstborn	Deu 21:15
Righteous and unrighteous judged	Isa 65:8
Righteous Branch	Jer 23:1
Righteous judgement of God	2 Ths 1:5
Righteous protected and blessed	Isa 58:8
Righteous will prosper	Psm 37:1
Righteousness Through Faith	Rom 3:21
Righteousness to all nations	Isa 61:10
Rights of an Apostle	1 Cor 9:1
Rights of marriage	1 Cor 7:1
Riot in Ephesus	Acts 19:23
Risen Christ	1 Pet 1:3
River flowing from the temple	Eze 47:1
River From the Temple	Eze 47:1
River of Life	Rev 22:1
Robbing God	Mal 3:6
Robe of the ephod	Ex 39:22
Rod becomes a serpent	Ex 7:8
Role of Christ in salvation	Heb 2:1
Rooms for Preparing Sacrifices	Eze 40:38
Rooms for Priests	Eze 40:44
Rooms for the Priests	Eze 42:1
Rout of Benjamin	Jud 20:29
Royal Line After the Exile	1 Chr 3:17
Ruin of Tyre foretold	Eze 27:25b
Rulers of Edom	Gen 36:31
Rulers of Edom	1 Chr 1:43

Ruler's daughter raised; a suffering woman healed	Mat 9:18 R
Ruler's daughter raised; a suffering woman healed	Luke 8:40 R
Rules for Christian Households	Col 3:18
Rules for Holy Living	Col 3:1
Rules for Priests	Lev 21:1
Ruth and Boaz at the Threshing Floor	Ruth 3:1
Ruth gleans in the field	Ruth 2:1
Ruth Meets Boaz	Ruth 2:1
Ruth refuses to leave Naomi	Ruth 1:15
Ruth visits Boaz	Ruth 3:6

S

Sabbath	Ex 31:12
Sabbath	Lev 23:3
Sabbath and jubilee years	Lev 25:1
Sabbath Laws	Ex 23:10
Sabbath observant stressed	Jer 17:19
Sabbath Offerings	Num 28:9
Sabbath reforms begun	Neh 13:15
Sabbath Regulations	Ex 35:1
Sabbath year of release	Deu 15:1
Sabbath-Breaker Put to Death	Num 15:32
Sabbath-Rest for the People of God	Heb 4:1
Sabbatical Year	Lev 25:1
Sacrifice at consecration	Ex 29:19
Sacrifice at one altar only	Deu 12:1
Sacrifice for an unknown murderer	Deu 21:1
Sacrifices in the temple	2 Chr 29:31
Sacrifices of deformed animals	Lev 22:17
Sacrificial feast of the LORD	Eze 39:25
Sadducees and the resurrection	Mat 22:23
Sadducees and the resurrection	Mark 12:18
Sadducees and the resurrection	Luke 20:27
Safety and joy under the Messiah	Isa 33:17
Saints in white robes	Rev 7:9
Salt and Light	Mat 5:13

Salutation	Eph 1:1
Salutation	Plip 1:1
Salutation	1 Tim 1:1
Salutation	2 Tim 1:1
Salutation	Titus 1:1
Salutation	Plem 1
Salutation	Jam 1:1
Salutation	1 Pet 1:1
Salutation	2 Pet 1:1
Salutation	2 John 1
Salutation	3 John 1
Salutation	Rev 1:4
Salutation and occasion of letter	Gal 1:1
Salutation and thanksgiving	Col 1:1
Salutation and thanksgiving	1 Ths 1:1
Salutation and thanksgiving	2 Ths 1:1
Salutation to the Book of Romans	Rom 1:1
Salvation for Others	Isa 56:1
Salvation through God's law	Psm 119:41
Samaria captured by Assyria	2 Kng 17:1
Samaria Resettled	2 Kng 17:24
Samaritan Opposition	Luke 9:51
Samson and Delilah	Jud 16:1
Samson and the woman of Timnah	Jud 14:1
Samson captured and imprisioned	Jud 16:18
Samson defeats the Philistines	Jud 15:9
Samson steals the city gates	Jud 16:1
Samson's Marriage	Jud 14:1
Samson's revenge and death	Jud 16:23
Samson's riddle at his wedding	Jud 14:10
Samson's Vengeance on the Philistines	Jud 15:1
Samuel addresses the people	1 Sam 12:1
Samuel Anoints David	1 Sam 16:1
Samuel Anoints Saul	1 Sam 9:1
Samuel born in answer to prayer	1 Sam 1:1
Samuel dedicated	1 Sam 1:21
Samuel delivers the LORD's sentence	1 Sam 15:17
Samuel ministers before the LORD	1 Sam 2:18
Samuel Rebukes Saul	1 Sam 13:1
Samuel's Farewell Speech	1 Sam 12:1
Samuel's sacrifice at Bethlehem	1 Sam 16:1

Sanctity of the priesthood	Lev 21:1
Satan permitted to tempt Job	Job 1:6
Satan's second request of God	Job 2:1
Saul among the prophets	1 Sam 10:9
Saul among the prophets	1 Sam 19:18
Saul and Samuel talk together	1 Sam 9:15
Saul and the medium at Endor	1 Sam 28:3
Saul and the Witch of Endor	1 Sam 28:1
Saul anointed by Samuel	1 Sam 10:1
Saul apologizes to David	1 Sam 26:17
Saul appears penitent	1 Sam 15:24
Saul becomes king of Israel	1 Sam 10:17
Saul comes to Samuel	1 Sam 9:1
Saul Confirmed as King	1 Sam 11:12
Saul has Ahimelech killed	1 Sam 22:11
Saul in Damascus and Jerusalem	Acts 9:19b
Saul killed on Mount Gilboa	1 Chr 10:1
Saul Kills the Priest of Nob	1 Sam 22:6
Saul Made King	1 Sam 10:9
Saul offers burnt offerings	1 Sam 13:8
Saul Pursues David	1 Sam 23:7
Saul Rescues the City of Jabesh	1 Sam 11:1
Saul Takes His Life	1 Sam 31:1
Saul Takes His Life	1 Chr 10:1
Saul Tries to Kill David	1 Sam 19:1
Saul tries to kill David	1 Sam 19:8
Saul wars against other nations	1 Sam 14:47
Saul's anger; Jonathan's warning	1 Sam 20:30
Saul's Conversion	Acts 9:1
Saul's disobedience	1 Sam 15:10
Saul's Family	1 Sam 14:49
Saul's Jealousy of David	1 Sam 18:1
Saul's Reign, 1050-1010 B.C.	1 Chr 8:29
Saul's seeming repentance	1 Sam 24:16
Saul's small army	1 Sam 13:15
Saved Soul is Grateful	Psm 116:1 M
Saving deeds of the LORD	1 Sam 12:6
Sayings of Agur	Pvb 30:1
Sayings of King Lemuel	Pvb 31:1
Sayings of the Wise	Pvb 22:17
Sayings of the wise	Pvb 24:23

Scapegoat	Lev 16:20
Scoffers to be scourged by Assyria	Isa 28:9
Scorn of idols	Psm 135:15
Scroll and the Lamb	Rev 5:1
Scroll and the Lamb	Rev 5:6
Sealing of God's servants	Rev 7:1
Sealing of the prophecy	Dan 12:5
Seals	Rev 6:1
Search for a queen	Est 2:1
Search for a wife for Isaac	Gen 24:1
Search for wisdom	Job 28:1
Second Census	Num 26:1
Second Day: firmament	Gen 1:6
Second Journey to Egypt	Gen 43:1
Second tables of stone	Ex 34:1
Second tables of stone	Deu 10:1
Second trip to Egypt	Gen 43:1
Secret of Samson's strength	Jud 16:15
Security of the godly	Psm 91:1
Selection of judges	Ex 18:13
Security of the righteous	Psm 37:23
Selection of temple servants	Ezra 8:15
Selection of Timothy	Acts 16:1
Self-Examination before Worship	Psm 26:1 M
Semites	1 Chr 1:17
Sending of the Messiah	Mal 2:17
Sennacherib murdered	2 Chr 32:16
Sennacherib taunts Hezekiah	Isa 36:1
Sennacherib taunts Jerusalem	2 Chr 32:9
Sennacherib Threatens Jerusalem	2 Kng 18:17
Sennacherib Threatens Jerusalem	2 Chr 32:1
Sennacherib Threatens Jerusalem	Isa 36:1
Sennacherib's Fall	Isa 37:21
Sentence against the Ammonites	Eze 21:28
Separation from foreigners	Neh 9:1
Separation of Abram and Lot	Gen 13:1
Separation of Paul and Barnabas	Acts 15:36
September, 1445 B.C.	Num 14:1
September, 444 B.C.	Neh 6:15
Sermon on the Mount: Beatitudes	Mat 5:1
Sermon on the plain	Luke 6:17

Servant and his master	1 Pet 2:18
Servant as seen by God	Isa 53:4
Servant as seen by man	Isa 53:1
Servant describes his errand	Gen 24:34
Servant of the LORD	Isa 42:1
Servant of the LORD	Isa 49:1
Servant's call and commission	Isa 49:1
Servant's exaltation	Isa 52:13
Serving the LORD and graven images	2 Kng 17:34
Setting Apart of the Levites	Num 8:5
Setting Up the Lamps	Num 8:1
Setting Up the Tabernacle	Ex 40:1
Settlement in Egypt	Gen 46:28
Settlement with an accuser	Luke 12:57
Seven Angels With Seven Plagues	Rev 15:1
Seven Bowls of God's Wrath	Rev 16:1
Seven bowls of wrath	Rev 15:1
Seven Woes	Mat 23:1
Seventh day: the Sabbath	Gen 2:1
Seventh seal	Rev 8:1
Seventh Seal and the Golden Censer	Rev 8:1
Seventh Trumpet	Rev 11:15
Seventh trumpet: the reign of Christ	Rev 11:15
Seventy "Sevens"	Dan 9:20
Seventy elders' prophecy	Num 11:24
Seventy Years of Captivity	Jer 25:1
Sexual Immorality	1 Cor 6:12
Shallum King of Israel	2 Kng 15:13
Shame of Moab	Jer 48:37
Shamgar	Jud 3:31
She of Him	Song 8:5a M
She Sings Again	Song 2:16 M
She Thinks Yearningly of Him	Song 1:12 M
She to Him	Song 8:6 M
Sheba is killed	2 Sam 20:14
Sheba leads Israel to revolt	2 Sam 20:1
Sheba Rebels Against David	2 Sam 20:1
Sheep and the Goats	Mat 25:31
Shepherd and His Flock	John 10:1
Shepherd psalm	Psm 23:1
Shepherd Struck, the Sheep Scattered	Zec 13:7

Shepherd, Guide and Host	Psm 23:1 M
Shepherds and Sheep	Eze 34:1
Shepherds and the Angels	Luke 2:8
Shime-i forgiven	2 Sam 19:16
Shime-i's broken oath and death	1 Kng 2:36
Shimei Curses David	2 Sam 16:5
Shining as Stars	Plip 2:12
Shipwreck	Acts 27:27
Shishak Attacks Jerusalem	2 Chr 12:1
Shortcomings of man	Ecc 7:15
Shrines and altars torn down	2 Kng 23:15
Shunammite promised a son	2 Kng 4:8
Shunammite woman comes home	2 Kng 8:1
Shunammite's Land Restored	2 Kng 8:1
Shunammite's Son Restored to Life	2 Kng 4:8
Sick healed; demons cast out	Mark 1:32
Sick healed; demons cast out	Luke 4:40
Sickness of Hezekiah	2 Kng 20:1
Sidon to perish	Eze 28:20
Siege and downfall of Jerusalem	Jer 52:1
Siege Lifted	2 Kng 7:3
Siege of Jericho	Jos 6:1
Siege of Jerusalem Symbolized	Eze 4:1
Siege of Nineveh	Nah 2:1
Sight of idols and abominations	Eze 8:7
Sign of Immanuel	Isa 7:1
Sign of Immanu-el	Isa 7:10
Sign of Jonah	Mat 12:38
Sign of Jonah	Luke 11:29
Sign of the good and bad figs	Jer 24:1
Signs for Moses	Ex 4:1
Signs of the end	Mat 24:32
Signs of the end	Mark 13:28
Signs of the end	Luke 21:25
Signs of the End of the Age	Mat 24:1
Signs of the End of the Age	Mark 13:1
Signs of the End of the Age	Luke 21:5
Silver Cup in a Sack	Gen 44:1
Silver Trumpets	Num 10:1
Simeon	1 Chr 4:24
Simon the Sorcerer	Acts 8:9

Sin and burnt offerings for priests	Lev 8:14
Sin and Doom of Godless Men	Jude 3
Sin and forgiveness	Mat 18:15
Sin and Punishment	Jer 8:4
Sin keeps Israel from deliverance	Isa 59:1
Sin of Lot's daughters	Gen 19:30
Sin of Oholah, Samaria	Eze 23:1
Sin of Oholibah, Jerusalem	Eze 23:11
Sin offering	Ex 29:10
Sin Offering	Lev 4:1
Sin Offering	Lev 6:24
Sin offering for a ruler	Lev 4:22
Sin offering for priest and people	Lev 16:11
Sin offering for the common people	Lev 4:27
Sin offering for the congregation	Lev 4:13
Sin offering for the priest	Lev 4:1
Sin offerings for the poor	Lev 5:7
Sin separates Israel from God	Isa 50:1
Sin, Confession and Redemption	Isa 59:1
Sin, Faith, Duty	Luke 17:1
Sinful reliance upon Egypt	Isa 30:1
Singers	1 Chr 25:1
Sinner's Cry for Forgiveness of Sin	Psm 130:1 M
Sins of Israel and Judah	2 Kng 17:7
Sins of Nineveh	Nah 3:1
Sins of Samaria	Amos 3:9
Sins of the people	Mal 3:6
Sins of the priesthood	Mal 1:6
Site, dimensions and materials	2 Chr 3:1
Six cities of refuge	Jos 20:1
Six of the seals opened	Rev 6:1
Six Woes	Luke 11:37
Sixth day: animals and man	Gen 1:24
Size and use of the altar	Eze 43:13
Slackness of Moab	Jer 48:10
Slander and false confidence	Jam 4:11
Slaughter by the sons of Levi	Ex 32:25
Slaughter of the idolaters	Eze 9:1
Slaughter of the inhabitants	Jos 8:24
Slaves and Masters	Eph 6:5
Slaves to Righteousness	Rom 6:15

Social Responsibility	Ex 22:16
Sodom and Gomorrah Destroyed	Gen 19:1
Sodom and Gomorrah destroyed	Gen 19:24
Sodom and Gomorrah to be destroyed	Gen 18:16
Sojourn in Moab	Ruth 1:1
Soldiers Mock Jesus	Mat 27:27
Soldiers Mock Jesus	Mark 15:16
Soldiers Mock Jesus	Luke 22:63
Solomon Acknowledged as King	1 Chr 29:21
Solomon anointed king	1 Kng 1:38
Solomon Asks for Wisdom	1 Kng 3:1
Solomon Asks for Wisdom	2 Chr 1:1
Solomon Builds His Palace	1 Kng 7:1
Solomon Builds the Temple	1 Kng 6:1
Solomon Builds the Temple	2 Chr 3:1
Solomon builds with forced labor	1 Kng 9:10
Solomon established in his kingdom	2 Chr 1:1
Solomon made king	1 Chr 29:22
Solomon takes foreign wives	1 Kng 11:1
Solomon to Ezra, 970-558 B.C.	1 Chr 3:10
Solomon uses forced labor	1 Kng 5:13
Solomon's Adversaries	1 Kng 11:14
Solomon's benediction	1 Kng 8:54
Solomon's buildings and cities	2 Chr 8:1
Solomon's Daily Provisions	1 Kng 4:20
Solomon's Death	1 Kng 11:41
Solomon's Death	2 Chr 9:29
Solomon's death and successor	2 Chr 9:29
Solomon's enemies: Hadad, Rezon	1 Kng 11:14
Solomon's great wisdom	1 Kng 4:29
Solomon's marriage alliance	1 Kng 3:1
Solomon's Officials and Governors	1 Kng 4:1
Solomon's Other Activities	1 Kng 9:10
Solomon's Other Activities	2 Chr 8:1
Solomon's Prayer of Dedication	1 Kng 8:22
Solomon's Prayer of Dedication	2 Chr 6:12
Solomon's speech	1 Kng 8:14
Solomon's Splendor	1 Kng 10:14
Solomon's Splendor	2 Chr 9:13
Solomon's Throne Established	1 Kng 2:13
Solomon's Wisdom	1 Kng 4:29

Solomon's wise decision	1 Kng 3:16
Solomon's Wives	1 Kng 11:1
Son Superior to Angels	Heb 1:1
Son's witness to the Father	John 5:19
Song for the distressed	Psm 56:1 R
Song of Confidence	Psm 144:1 M
Song of confidence in God	Psm 108:1 R
Song of confidence in God	Psm 123:1 R
Song of Deborah	Jud 5:1
Song of Mary	Luke 1:46b
Song of Miriam	Ex 15:19
Song of Moses	Ex 15:1
Song of Moses	Deu 31:30
Song of praise	Psm 22:22 R
Song of Praise	Isa 26:1
Song of praise and assurance	Psm 69:29
Song of praise and joy	Psm 100:1 R
Song of Praise to the LORD	Isa 42:10
Song of rejoicing in Judah	Isa 26:1
Song of remembrance	Psm 106:1 R
Song of Simeon	Luke 2:29
Song of the humble	Psm 131:1 R
Song of the Redeemed	Psm 107:1 M
Song of the Vineyard	Isa 5:1
Song of Zechariah	Luke 1:67
Song to Mount Zion	Psm 48:1 R
Song to the King of glory	Psm 24:1
Song to Zechariah	Luke 1:14
Songs of Praise	Isa 12:1
Sons of Aaron	Num 3:1
Sons of Bilhah and Zilpah	Gen 30:1
Sons of David	1 Chr 3:1
Sons of Gershon	Num 4:21
Sons of God	Gal 3:26
Sons of Kohath	Num 4:1
Sons of Merari	Num 4:29
Sons of Noah	Gen 9:18
Sons of Seir	Gen 36:20
Sons of Shem	Gen 10:21
Sorrow of separation	Psm 42:1
Soul that sins shall die	Eze 18:1

Soul Thirsting for God	Psm 63:1 M
Soul Who Sins Will Die	Eze 18:1
Soul's Longing for God	Psm 42:1 M
Source of beauty and pleasure	Ecc 3:10
Source of great wealth	Pvb 13:1
Source of hope	Pvb 13:12
Source of love	1 John 4:7
Source of the revelation	Rev 1:1
Source of true wisdom	Job 28:12
South Gate	Eze 40:24
Southern Cities Conquered	Jos 10:29
Sowing Generously	2 Cor 9:6
Span of a life	Ecc 12:1
Specific gifts	1 Cor 12:27
Speech by Solomon	2 Chr 6:1
Speech of Eliphaz	Job 4:1
Spies return	Num 13:25
Spies Sent Out	Deu 1:19
Spiritual Blessings in Christ	Eph 1:3
Spiritual blessings through Christ	Eph 1:3
Spiritual Blindness	John 9:35
Spiritual Gifts	1 Cor 12:1
Splendor and success of the king	Psm 21:1
Spying of the Midianite camp	Jud 7:9
Stages in Israel's Journey	Num 33:1
Stand Firm	2 Ths 2:13
Stand in Awe of God	Ecc 5:1
Statement of present complaints	Psm 44:9
Steadfast love of the LORD	Psm 103:15
Stephen Seized	Acts 6:8
Stephen's Speech to the Sanhedrin	Acts 7:1
Stoning and death of Stephen	Acts 7:54
Stoning of Achan	Jos 7:16
Stoning of Stephen	Acts 7:54
Stoning the Sabbath breaker	Num 15:32
Stopover at Malta	Acts 28:1
Storm	Acts 27:13
Storm at Sea	Acts 27:13
Storm stilled	Mat 8:23
Storm stilled	Mark 4:35
Storm stilled	Luke 8:22

Strength of love	Song 8:5b
Strength of the Behemoth	Job 40:15
Strength through the Spirit	Eph 3:14
Struggling With Sin	Rom 7:7
Stubborn Israel	Isa 48:1
Submission to Rulers and Masters	1 Pet 2:13
Submission to the Authorities	Rom 13:1
Submit Yourselves to God	Jam 4:1
Subsiding of the waters	Gen 8:1
Sudden coming of the Lord	1 Ths 5:1
Suffering and Glory of the Servant	Isa 52:13
Suffering for Being a Christian	1 Pet 4:12
Suffering for Doing Good	1 Pet 3:8
Suffering ministry	2 Cor 6:1 R
Sufferings of the psalmist	Psm 102:1
Sufficiency of Christ	Col 2:8
Summary of Jehu's reign	2 Kng 10:28
Summary of Jesus' claims	John 12:44 R
Summary of Rehoboam's reign	2 Chr 12:13
Summary of the covenant	Neh 10:28
Summer, 444 B.C.	Neh 2:11
Summons to invade Judah	Jer 5:10
Summons to repentance	Jer 3:21
Summons to surrender	Isa 36:11
Sun Stands Still	Jos 10:1
Sun stands still	Jos 10:12
Superiority of Christ's priesthood	Heb 7:15
Superiority of the new covenant	Heb 8:1
Supplementary Offerings	Num 15:1
Support of the priesthood begun	Neh 13:10
Supremacy of Christ	Col 1:15
Supremacy of God's people	Isa 60:10
Sure destruction	Nah 3:8
Swarms of flies	Ex 8:20
Sword sharpened	Eze 21:8
Sword wielded by Babylon	Eze 21:18
Symbol of the fall of Jerusalem	Eze 5:1
Symbol of the famine	Eze 4:9
Symbol of the siege and exile	Eze 4:1
Syrians and Ammonites flee	2 Sam 10:6
Syrians flee	2 Kng 7:3

Tabernacle	Ex 26:1
Tabernacle	Ex 36:8
Tabernacle frames made	Ex 36:20
Tabernacle furnishings	Ex 26:7
Tabitha raised from the dead	Acts 9:36
Table	Ex 25:23
Table	Ex 37:10
Table and the lampstand	Ex 37:10
Table of Nations	Gen 10:1
Tablets Like the First Ones	Deu 10:1
Tamar's mourning	2 Sam 13:15
Taming the Tongue	Jam 3:1
Taskmasters increase Israel's work	Ex 5:10
Tassels of remembrance	Num 15:37
Tassels on Garments	Num 15:37
Tattenai's Letter to Darius	Ezra 5:1
Tattenai's letter to Darius	Ezra 5:6
Taunt against the king of Babylon	Isa 14:1
Taxes to Caesar	Mark 12:13
Taxes to Caesar	Luke 20:19
Teaching about anxiety	Luke 12:22
Teaching about discipleship	Mat 8:18
Teaching about discipleship	Luke 9:57
Teaching about judging others	Luke 6:37
Teaching about salt and light	Mat 5:13
Teaching on faith and forgiveness	Luke 17:1
Teaching on marriage and divorce	Mat 19:1
Teaching on marriage and divorce	Mark 10:1
Teaching on the kingdom of God	Mark 10:23
Teaching on the kingdom of heaven	Mat 19:23
Temple	Eze 40:48
Temple Musicians	1 Chr 6:31
Temple rebuilt and dedicated	Ezra 6:13
Temple Tax	Mat 17:24
Temple's Furnishings	1 Kng 7:13
Temple's Furnishings	2 Chr 4:1
Temporary sacrifices by Levites	Heb 9:1
Temptation in the wilderness	Mat 4:1
Temptation in the wilderness	Luke 4:1

Temptation of Jesus	Mat 4:1
Temptation of Jesus	Luke 4:1
Ten Commandments	Ex 20:1
Ten Commandments	Deu 5:1
Ten Healed of Leprosy	Luke 17:11
Ten sons report to Jacob	Gen 42:29
Tent of Meeting	Ex 33:7
Terrible days to come	Jer 7:30
Test for a suspected adulterer	Num 5:23
Test for an Unfaithful Wife	Num 5:5
Test of belief	1 John 2:18
Test of Daniel and his friends	Dan 1:8
Test of false prophets	Mat 7:15
Test of love	1 John 2:7
Test of righteousness	1 John 1:5
Test the Spirits	1 John 4:1
Testimonies About Jesus	John 5:31
Testimony of Paul	1 Tim 1:12
Thanks for Blessings	Psm 111:1 M
Thanks for Their Gifts	Plip 4:10
Thanks to God for His Church	Psm 84:1 M
Thanks to God, the Righteous Judge	Psm 75:1 M
Thanksgiving	Rom 1:8
Thanksgiving	1 Cor 1:4
Thanksgiving and appeal	2 Ths 2:13
Thanksgiving and Petition	Psm 108:1 M
Thanksgiving and Prayer	Eph 1:15
Thanksgiving and Prayer	Plip 1:3
Thanksgiving and Prayer	Col 1:3
Thanksgiving and Prayer	2 Ths 1:3
Thanksgiving and Prayer	Plem 4
Thanksgiving for God's deliverance	Psm 124:1
Thanksgiving for God's salvation	Isa 12:1
Thanksgiving for the Thessalonians' Faith	1 Ths 1:2
The way, the truth and the life	John 14:1
Their Reply	Song 5:9 M
Theme	Rom 1:16
Theme: vanity of human wisdom	Ecc 1:1
Third day: dry land and vegetation	Gen 1:9
Third year tithe	Deu 26:12
Thirsty soul	Psm 63:1

Thomas' doubt and belief	John 20:24
Those Guilty of Intermarriage	Ezra 10:18
Those who signed the covenant	Neh 9:38
Thoughts in the night	Psm 4:1
Thousand Years	Rev 20:1
Threat of Captivity	Jer 13:15
Threat of exile	Jer 16:1
Threat of further plagues	Ex 9:13
Three Angels	Rev 14:6
Three Annual Festivals	Ex 23:14
Three Visitors	Gen 18:1
Throne in Heaven	Rev 4:1
Through Macedonia and Greece	Acts 20:1
Time and circumstances of the coming	2 Pet 3:8
Time for Everything	Ecc 3:1
Time of great trouble	Dan 12:1
Time of tribulation	Mat 24:15
Time of tribulation	Mark 13:14
Timothy and Epaphroditus	Plip 2:19
Timothy Joins Paul and Silas	Acts 16:1
Timothy urged to pray	1 Tim 1:18
Timothy's Encouraging Report	1 Ths 3:6
Timothy's visit and report	1 Ths 3:1
Tired ministry	2 Cor 4:7 R
Tithe for the Levites	Num 18:21
Tithes	Deu 14:22
Titus Sent to Corinth	2 Cor 8:16
Titus' Task on Crete	Titus 1:5
To Elders and Young Men	1 Pet 5:1
To God alone belongs glory	Psm 115:1
To God Alone the Glory	Psm 115:1 M
To Noah's Sons	1 Chr 1:1
To the Church in Ephesus	Rev 2:1
To the Church in Laodicea	Rev 3:14
To the Church in Pergamum	Rev 2:12
To the Church in Philadelphia	Rev 3:7
To the Church in Sardis	Rev 3:1
To the Church in Smyrna	Rev 2:8
To the Church in Thyatira	Rev 2:18
To Us a Child Is Born	Isa 9:1
Tobiah's furniture cast out	Neh 13:4

Toil and enjoyment	Ecc 5:13
Toil is Meaningless	Ecc 2:17
Toil of the wise and the foolish	Ecc 4:4
Tola	Jud 10:1
Tola and Jair judge Israel	Jud 10:1
Tomb sealed and guarded	Mat 27:62
Tongue of the wise	Pvb 15:1
Torment of separation	Song 5:2
Tower of Babel	Gen 11:1
Tower of Shechem burned	Jud 9:46
Towns for the Levites	Num 35:1
Towns for the Levites	Jos 21:1
Tradition of the elders	Mat 15:1
Tradition of the elders	Mark 7:1
Transfiguration	Mat 17:1
Transfiguration	Mark 9:1
Transfiguration	Mark 9:2
Transfiguration	Luke 9:28
Transjordon Tribes	Num 32:1
Treachery of Ahithophel	2 Sam 15:30
Treachery of the Ziphites	1 Sam 23:19
Treasurers and Other Officials	1 Chr 26:20
Treasures in Heaven	Mat 6:19
Treasures in Jars of Clay	2 Cor 4:1
Treasures of the wicked	Pvb 21:1
Treasures of the wise	Pvb 21:13
Treaty at Beersheba	Gen 21:22
Tree and Its Fruit	Mat 7:15
Tree and Its Fruit	Luke 6:43
Trial Before Felix	Acts 24:1
Trial Before Festus	Acts 25:1
Trials and Temptations	Jam 1:2
Trials of the apostles	1 Cor 4:8
Tribes and their sizes	Num 1:17
Tribute to John the Baptist	Mat 11:2
Tribute to John the Baptist	Luke 7:18
Trickery of the Gibeonites	Jos 9:1
Triumph of the Jews	Est 9:1
Triumph of the king	Psm 2:7
Triumph of the resurrection	1 Cor 15:51
Triumph over enemies	Psm 59:1

Triumphal Entry	Mat 21:1
Triumphal Entry	Mark 11:1
Triumphal Entry	Luke 19:28
Triumphal Entry	John 12:12
Triumphant ministry	2 Cor 2:12 R
Triumphs of the king	Psm 18:31
True and false religion	Psm 50:1
True and false wisdom	Jam 3:13
True and false worship	Isa 66:1
True believers encouraged	Heb 6:9
True center of Christian life	Col 3:1
True children of Abraham	John 8:31
True discipleship	Mark 9:33
True discipleship	Luke 9:46
True faith evidenced by words	Jam 3:1
True faith evidenced by works	Jam 2:14
True faith impartial	Jam 2:1
True Fasting	Isa 58:1
True Godliness	Psm 50:1 M
True religion evidenced by conduct	Jam 1:19
True religion patient in temptation	Jam 1:2
True wisdom is knowing the LORD	Jer 9:23
True wisdom the gift of God	1 Cor 2:6
True Worshiper of the King of Glory	Psm 24:1 M
Trumpets	Rev 8:6
Trust God in the Evening	Psm 4:1 M
Trust God in the morning	Psm 3:1 M
Trust in false wisdom	Jer 8:4
Trust in God's salvation	Mic 7:7
Trustworthy and the talebearer	Pvb 11:12
Twelve Apostles	Luke 6:12
Twelve curses at Mount Ebal	Deu 27:15
Twelve spies sent to Canaan	Num 13:1
Twelve stones of memorial	Jos 4:1
Two Adulterous Sisters	Eze 23:1
Two Baskets of Figs	Jer 24:1
Two Blind Men Receive Sight	Mat 20:29
Two Eagles and a Vine	Eze 17:1
Two Kinds of Life; Two Destinies	Psm 73:1 M
Two Kinds of Wisdom	Jam 3:13
Two Shepherds	Zec 11:4

Two silver trumpets	Num 10:1
Two spies sent to Jericho	Jos 2:1
Two Witnesses	Rev 11:1
Tyre's pride and ruin	Eze 28:1

U

Unacceptable Sacrifices	Lev 22:17
Unbelief of the Jewish Leaders	John 7:45
Unbelief of the Jews	John 10:22
Unbelief of the people	Eze 12:1
Uncertainty of wisdom	Ecc 1:12
Unclean spirit cast out	Mark 1:21
Unclean spirit cast out	Luke 4:31
Uncleanness in the Camp	Deu 23:9
Unfaithful Israel	Jer 3:6
Unfaithfulness of Judah	Jer 35:12
Ungodly rulers to be punished	Eze 11:1
Unity in diversity	1 Cor 12:12
Unity in the Body of Christ	Eph 4:1
Unity of the Spirit	Eph 4:1
Unjust judgements rebuked	Psm 82:1
Unlawful sexual relations	Lev 18:1
Unlimited mercy of God	Jon 4:1
Upright and the wicked	Pvb 14:1
Upward call of God	Plip 3:12
Uriah's murder	Jer 26:20
Use of spiritual gifts	1 Cor 14:26
Use of wealth	1 Tim 6:17
Uselessness of the false prophets	Lam 4:13
Uzziah King of Judah	2 Chr 26:1
Uzziah's sin, punishment and death	2 Chr 26:16

V

Validity of Jesus' Testimony	John 8:12
Valley of Dry Bones	Eze 37:1
Valley of Slaughter	Jer 7:30
Valuable metals used	Ex 38:24
Value of a good name	Pvb 22:1
Value of life	Mat 10:26

Value of life	Luke 12:1
Value of wisdom over wealth	Ecc 7:10
Vanity of all life	Ecc 3:16
Vanity of hope	Ecc 6:7
Vanity of pleasure and wealth	Ecc 2:1
Vanity of riches	Ecc 5:8
Vanity of vows	Ecc 5:1
Vanity of wealth and honor	Ecc 6:1
Vanity of work without God	Psm 127:1
Varieties of gifts	1 Cor 12:1
Various Laws	Lev 19:1
Various Laws	Deu 21:22
Veiling of women	1 Cor 11:1
Vengeance of the LORD	Jer 25:30
Vengeance on the Midianites	Num 31:1
Version of the four creatures	Eze 1:1
Vestibule and its furnishings	Eze 40:38
Victories over the Philistines	2 Sam 21:15
Victorious power of God	Psm 76:1
Victory and the fiery serpents	Num 21:2
Victory of the Jews	Est 8:15
Victory over Og	Deu 3:1
Victory over Sihon	Deu 2:26
Victory over the Ammonites	2 Sam 10:15
Victory over the Ammonites	2 Sam 12:26
Victory through faith	1 John 5:1
Villages outside Jerusalem	Neh 11:25
Vine and the Branches	John 15:1
Virtuous woman	Pvb 31:10
Vision in the temple	Eze 8:1
Vision of dry bones in the valley	Eze 37:1
Vision of Israel's ruin	Amos 8:1
Vision of Obadiah	Obd 1:1
Vision of the four wheels	Eze 1:15
Vision of the plumb line	Amos 7:7
Vision of the ram, goat and horn	Dan 8:1
Visit of the Magi	Mat 2:1
Visit of the Queen of Sheba	1 Kng 10:1
Visit of the Queen of Sheba	2 Chr 9:1
Visit to Babylon	Eze 3:16
Voice and the vision	Rev 1:9

Vows	Num 30:1
Vows involving animals	Lev 27:9
Vows involving house and land	Lev 27:14
Vows involving persons	Lev 27:1

W

Wailing over Jerusalem's ruin	Jer 9:10
Waiting for God in silence	Psm 62:1
Waiting on the LORD	Psm 130:1
Walk to Emmaus	Luke 24:13
Walking in the Light	1 John 1:5
Walking in the way of wisdom	Pvb 2:16
Wanderings in the Desert	Deu 2:1
War between Abijah and Jeroboam	2 Chr 13:13
War between Judah and Israel	1 Kng 15:16
War between Judah and Israel	2 Chr 25:17
War Between the Houses of David and Saul	2 Sam 2:8
War with Ammonites and Philistines	1 Chr 20:1
War with the Amalekites	1 Sam 15:1
War with the Philistines	1 Sam 13:1
War With the Philistines	1 Chr 20:4
Warning about defilement	Lev 18:24
Warning Against Adultery	Pvb 5:1
Warning Against Adultery	Pvb 6:20
Warning Against Antichrists	1 John 2:18
Warning against apostasy	Heb 6:1
Warning against apostasy	Heb 13:7
Warning Against Falling Away	Heb 5:11
Warning against false teachers	1 Tim 6:2b
Warning Against False Teachers of the Law	1 Tim 1:3
Warning against heathen idolatry	Ex 34:11
Warning against idolatry	Deu 12:29
Warning against neglect of wisdom	Pvb 1:20
Warning against Pharisaism	Mat 23:1
Warning against Pharisaism	Luke 11:37
Warning against pride	Deu 8:11
Warning Against Refusing God	Heb 12:14
Warning Against Rejecting Wisdom	Pvb 1:20
Warning against scribes	Luke 20:45
Warning against seeking signs	Mat 12:38

Warning against seeking signs	Luke 11:29
Warning against seven sins	Pvb 6:16
Warning against sowing discord	Pvb 6:12
Warning Against the Adulteress	Pvb 7:1
Warning Against Unbelief	Heb 3:7
Warning against unchastity	Pvb 5:1
Warning of Coming Destruction	Zep 1:2
Warning to Israel	Eze 3:16
Warning to Pay Attention	Heb 2:1
Warning to Rich Oppressors	Jam 5:1
Warning to the priesthood	Mal 2:1
Warning to the unfaithful	Mal 2:10
Warning to Zedekiah	Jer 34:1
Warnings against debt and idleness	Pvb 6:1
Warnings Against Folly	Pvb 6:1
Warnings against violence	Pvb 1:10
Warnings and Encouragements	Luke 12:1
Warnings From Israel's History	1 Cor 10:1
Warrior's psalm	Psm 144:1
Warriors Join David	1 Chr 12:1
Wars Against the Philistines	2 Sam 21:15
Wars of the kings	Gen 14:1
Washing the disciples's feet	John 13:1
Watched over with wisdom	Pvb 24:3
Watchfulness	Luke 12:35
Water and tree of life	Rev 22:1
Water becomes blood	Ex 7:14
Water for Cleansing	Num 19:1
Water from the rock	Ex 17:1
Water From the Rock	Num 20:1
Water from the rock	Num 20:2
Waters of Marah and Elim	Ex 15:22
Way of love	1 Cor 12:31b
Way of wicked men	Job 22:12
Ways of a king	1 Sam 8:10
Weak and the Strong	Rom 14:1
Wealth and wisdom of Solomon	2 Chr 9:13
Wealth in wisdom	Pvb 10:1
Weeping and Mourning	Mic 1:8
Welcome to the Lovers	Song 5:1b M
What defiles a man	Mat 15:10

130

What defiles a man	Mark 7:14
What God declares comes to pass	Isa 48:1
What Must Be Taught to Various Groups	Titus 2:1
What the LORD requires	Mic 6:1
When judgement is delayed	Psm 10:1
Where is there hope?	Job 17:3
Who Is the Greatest?	Mark 9:33
Who Will Be the Greatest?	Luke 9:46
Whoever Is Not Against Us Is for Us	Mark 9:38
Whole armor of God	Eph 6:10
Whole duty of man	Ecc 12:9
Whose Son Is the Christ?	Mat 22:41
Whose Son Is the Christ?	Mark 12:35
Whose Son Is the Christ?	Luke 20:41
Why the LORD punished Israel	Deu 32:19
Wicked and the righteous	Pvb 28:1
Wicked deeds of the rich	Mic 2:1
Wicked destroy the righteous	Hab 1:12
Wicked ways of men	Pvb 16:25
Wicked who repent shall live	Eze 18:21
Wicked wither away	Job 24:13
Wickedness confronts God's love	Psm 36:1
Wickedness of Joash	2 Chr 24:17
Wickedness of Mankind	Psm 14:1 M
Widow's Offering	Mark 12:41
Widow's Offering	Luke 21:1
Widow's Oil	2 Kng 4:1
Widow's penny	Mark 12:41
Wilderness of Shur	Ex 15:22
Wilderness of Sin	Ex 16:1
Wilderness of Sinai	Ex 19:1
Window at Zarephath	1 Kng 17:7
Window's jar of oil	2 Kng 4:1
Wineskins	Jer 13:12
Wisdom	Ecc 7:1
Wisdom and Folly Are Meaningless	Ecc 2:12
Wisdom and folly contrasted	Pvb 9:1
Wisdom and folly contrasted	Ecc 7:19
Wisdom Better Than Folly	Ecc 9:13
Wisdom for today and tomorrow	Pvb 27:1
Wisdom From the Spirit	1 Cor 2:6

131

Wisdom Is Meaningless	Ecc 1:12
Wisdom Is Supreme	Pvb 4:1
Wisdom more precious than wealth	Pvb 3:9
Wisdom the fountain of life	Pvb 16:12
Wisdom's Call	Pvb 8:1
Wise and Foolish Builders	Mat 7:24
Wise and Foolish Builders	Luke 6:46
Wise and the foolish	Pvb 12:15
Wise inherit honor	Pvb 3:21
Wise man and the fool	Ecc 10:1
Wise Ruling	1 Kng 3:16
Wise words to a son	Pvb 23:15
Withered Fig Tree	Mark 11:20
Witness of the prophets	1 Pet 1:10
Witnesses	Deu 19:15
Witnesses Summoned Against Israel	Amos 3:1
Wives and Husbands	Eph 5:22
Wives and Husbands	1 Pet 3:1
Wives for the Benjaminites	Jud 21:1
Wives for the Benjaminites	Jud 21:16
Woe and derision to Ephraim	Hos 7:8
Woe on Unrepentant Cities	Mat 11:20
Woe to David's City	Isa 29:1
Woe to Ephraim	Isa 28:1
Woe to Nineveh	Nah 3:1
Woe to the Complacent	Amos 6:1
Woe to the Obstinate Nation	Isa 30:1
Woe to the unrighteous	Hab 2:6
Woe to Those Who Rely on Egypt	Isa 31:1
Woe upon Jerusalem	Zep 3:1
Woe upon the drunkards of Ephraim	Isa 28:1
Woe upon the nations	Zep 2:5
Woes and Judgements	Isa 5:8
Woes upon the Pharisees	Mat 23:13
Woman and the Dragon	Rev 12:1
Woman caught in adultery	John 8:1
Woman healed on the Sabbath	Luke 13:10 R
Woman in a Basket	Zec 5:5
Woman on the Beast	Rev 17:1
Women of Jerusalem	Isa 32:9
Wonders of animal life	Job 38:39

Word Became Flesh	John 1:1
Word of Life	1 John 1:1
Words of Huldah the prophetess	2 Kng 22:14
Words of thanks to Philemon	Plem 4
Words of the wise and the foolish	Pvb 18:1
Work of the Holy Spirit	John 16:5
Work stopped in Jerusalem	Ezra 4:17
Workers Are Few	Mat 9:35
Workman Approved by God	2 Tim 2:14
Workman approved of God	2 Tim 2:14 R
Workmen gathered	Ex 35:30
Works and word of God	Psm 19:1
Works of light and darkness	Eph 5:1
World Hates the Disciples	John 15:18
World Praise to God	Psm 117:1 M
World: guilty before God	Rom 3:9
Worship in the Earthly Tabernacle	Heb 9:1
Worshiping Other Gods	Deu 13:1
Worshiping Other Gods	Deu 16:21
Writing on the scroll	Jer 36:1
Writing on the Wall	Dan 5:1
Writings of Jeremiah	Jer 51:59

Y

Year for Canceling Debts	Deu 15:1
Year of Jubilee	Lev 25:8
Year of redemption	Isa 63:1
Year of the LORD's Favor	Isa 61:1
Years in the wilderness	Deu 2:1
Years of the Pharisees and Herod	Mark 8:14
Yeast of the Pharisees and Sadducees	Mat 16:5
Yoke of bondage broken	Jer 30:1

Z

Zacchaeus the Tax Collector	Luke 19:1
Zebah and Zalmunna	Jud 8:1
Zebah and Zalmunna killed	Jud 8:13
Zechariah King of Israel	2 Kng 15:8
Zechariah's Song	Luke 1:67

Zedekiah King of Judah	2 Kng 24:18
Zedekiah King of Judah	2 Chr 36:11
Zedekiah Questions Jeremiah Again	Jer 38:14
Zedekiah reigns; Jerusalem besieged	2 Kng 24:18
Zedekiah's broken promise	Jer 34:1
Zedekiah's prayer; God's answer	Jer 21:1
Zelophehad's Daughters	Num 27:1
Zerubbabel begins to build again	Ezra 5:1
Zerubbabel the LORD's Signet Ring	Hag 2:20
Zerubbabel, the servant of the LORD	Hag 2:20
Ziba's lie	2 Sam 16:1
Zimri King of Israel	1 Kng 16:15
Zion assured of God's love	Isa 49:14
Zion's New Name	Isa 62:1
Zion's refuge in God	Psm 102:12
Ziphites betray David	1 Sam 26:1
Zophar	Job 11:1
Zophar	Job 20:1
Zophar accuses Job of guilt	Job 11:1
Zophar's speech on the wicked	Job 20:1

Curious Facts

Airplane	Isa 31:5
Automobile	Nah 2:4
Avoid Foolish Questions	2 Tim 2:23; Tit 3:9
Brawling Woman	Pvb 25:24
Bride (Church)	Rev 22:17
Bridegroom (Jesus)	Mat 25:1-14
Brothers of Jesus	Mark 6:3
Camel through the eye of a needle	Mat 19:24
Cannibalism	Lev 26:29
Cucumbers, melons, leeks, onions, garlic all in the same verse	Num 11:5
Druggist (Apothecary)	Ex 30:35
Electa (Elect Lady)	2 John 1
Father of 88 Children	2 Chr 11:21
Frying Pan	Lev 2:7
Garments Not to be Exchanged	Deu 22:5
Hired Razor	Isa 7:20
Ideal Woman	Pvb 31:10-31
Iron Bedstead	Deu 3:11
Iron Pen	Job 37:18
Last Time Moses Seen	Mat 17:3
Longest Verse in Bible	Est 8:9
Longest Word in Bible	Isa 8:1
Looking Glass	Job 37:18
Man First Shaves Self	Gen 41:14
Man Wiping Dishes	2 Kng 21:13
Meshach, Shadrach, Abednego	Dan 3:26
Middle verse in Bible	Psm 118:8
Pen of Iron With Diamond Point	Jer 17:1
Penknife	Jer 36:23
Pick Corn (Not Cut)	Deu 23:25
Preaching (On Radio)	Luke 12:3
Radio	Job 38:35
Revenge Forbidden	Rom 12:17-19

Second Death	Rev 20:11-15
Seven Hundred Left Handed Men	Jud 20:16
Seven Women Want the Same Man	Isa 4:1
Seven Things Hateful to God	Pvb 6:16-20
Shortest Verse in Old Testament	1 Chr 1:25
Shortest Verse in New Testament	John 11:35
Submarine	Job 41:14-32
Tattooing Forbidden	Lev 19:28
Telephone	Job 38:35
Term Easter Used	Acts 12:4
Townclerk	Acts 19:35
Unpardonable Sin	Mt 12:31;
	Mk 3:29;
	Heb 6:4-6,
	10:26-34
Ventriloquism	Isa 29:4
Verse Containing All Letters of Alphabet Except J	Ezra 7:21
Wayfaring Men	Isa 35:8;
	Jer 14:8
Weather Forecast	Luke 12:54-57
Who Shall Not Go To Heaven	1 Cor 6:9-10
Woman First Paints Face	2 Kng 9:30

Favorite Readings

A Prayer of Forgiveness	Psm 51
A Promise for Faithfulness	Pvb 3:1-6
Assurance of God's Mercy	Psm 40:1-5
Banishing Fear of Death	John 11:25
Christ Teaches Forgiveness	Mat 18:21-35
Confidence in God	Psm 37
Does God Figure in Our National Life?	Deu 8
Duties of Children	Eph 6:1-2

For a Stirring Record Of What Trust in God Can Do	Heb 11
For Inward Peace	John 14
For the Way of Prayer	Eph 3
From Death unto Life	John 5:24
God Is Our Refuge and Strength	Psm 46
God's Eternal Mercy	Psm 103
Gospel of Christ	Rom 1:16
Hope in Time of Trouble	Psm 42
If You Are Bored	Job 38-40; Psm 103-104
If You Are Facing a Crisis	Psm 46
If You Are Having To Put Up A Stiff Fight	Ephesians
If You Are Satisfied With Being Well-to-Do	Luke 15-16
If You Are Sick or in Pain	Psm 91
If You Have a Fear of Death	John 11, 17, 20 2 Cor 4,5; Rev 21
If You Have Been Bereaved	1 Cor 15; Rev 21
If You Have Experienced Severe Losses	Rom 8
Jesus' Mission	Luke 19:10
Jesus' New Commandment	John 13:34
Living Successfully With Others	Rom 12
Love Chapter	1 Cor 13
Opening the Door to Jesus	Rev 3:20
Promise of Eternal Life	John 3:16
Resurrection through Jesus	1 Cor 15
Searching the Scriptures	John 5:39
Setting a Good Example	Mat 5:16
Spiritual Peace	John 14
The Beatitudes	Mat 5:3-11
The Best Investment is Described	Mat 6
The Birth of Jesus	Luke 2

The Choice of Treasure   Mat 6:19-34
The Christian's Armor   Eph 5:11-17
The Christian's Hope   Rom 8:31-39
The Crown of Life   Rev 2:10
The Crucifixion   John 19
The Golden Rule   Mat 7:12
The Good Samaritan   Luke 10:30-37
The Great Commandments   Mat 22:35-40
The Heroes of the Faith   Heb 11
The House Built Upon a Rock   Mat 7:24-27
The Last Judgement   Mat 25:31-46
The Lord's Prayer   Mat 6:9-13
The Love of Christ   Eph 3:14-21
The Prodigal Son   Luke 15:11-32
The Promise of the Gospel   Isa 40
The Resurrection   Mat 28
The Return for Good Deeds   Luke 6:38
The Sermon on the Mount   Mat 5-7
The Shepherd's Psalm   Psm 23
The Ten Commandments   Ex 20:3-17
The Value of the Scriptures   2 Tim 3
The Way to Salvation   Rom 10:9
To Live Successfully With Your
   Fellowman   Rom 12
Treatment of Others   Eph 4:32
Two Types of Prayer   Luke 18:9-14
What We Shall Reap   Gal 6:7
When Business Is Poor   Psm 37
When Everything Seems to be
   Going From Bad to Worse   2 Tim 3
When God Seems Far Away   Psm 139
When Tempted to do Wrong   Psm 139
When Things Look Blue   Isa 40
When You Are Anxious For
   Dear Ones   Psm 107
When You Are Discouraged   Psm 23
When You Are Lonely or Fearful   Psm 27

When You Are Very Weary	Mat 11:28-30; Rom 8:31-39
When You Have Been Placed In a Position of Great Responsibility	Jos 1
When You Leave Home For Work or Travel	Psm 121
When You Plan Your Budget	Luke 19
Wise and Foolish Virgins	Mat 25:1-13
Withstanding Temptation	Psm 1

The Life of Our Lord Jesus

Birth of John the Baptist Foretold	Luke 1:5
Birth of Jesus Foretold	Mt 1:18; Lk 1:26
Birth and Naming of John	Luke 1:39
Birth of Jesus	Lk 2:1; Jn 1:1-14
Genealogies of Jesus	Mt 1:1; Lk 3:23
Circumcision and Naming of Jesus	Luke 2:21
Presentation of Jesus in the Temple	Luke 2:22
Coming of the Wise Men	Mt 2:1
Flight to—Return from Egypt	Mt 2:19
The Lad Jesus in the Temple	Luke 2:41
John the Baptist's Ministry	Mt 3:1; Mk 1:1; Lk 3:1; Jn 1:6,15
The Baptism of Jesus	Mt 3:13; Mk 1:9; Lk 3:21
The Temptation of Jesus	Mt 4:1; Mk 1:12; Lk 4:1
Jesus Begins His Ministry	Mt 4:12; Mk 1:14; Lk 4:14
John's Witness of Jesus	John 1:15
Call of First Disciples	Mt 4:18; Mk 1:16; Lk 5:1; Jn 1:35
Jesus' Sermon on the Mount	Mt 5, 6, 7; Lk 6:17
Jesus' First Miracle	John 2:1
Jesus at Jerusalem	John 2:13
Nicodemus Visits Jesus	John 3:1

The Twelve	Mt 10:2; Mk 3:13; Lk 6:13
The Twelve Commissioned and Sent Forth	Mt 10:1; Mk 3:13; Lk 9:1
The Twelve Return	Mk 6:30; Lk 9:10
John the Baptist's Death	Mt 14:1; Mk 6:14; Lk 9:7
Peter's Confession of Christ	Mt 16:13; Mk 8:27; Lk 9:18
Jesus Foretells His Own Death	Mt 16:21; Mk 8:31; Lk 9:22
The Transfiguration (of Jesus)	Mt 17:1; Mk 9:2; Lk 9:28
The Seventy Sent Out: Their Return	Luke 10:1
The Raising of Lazarus	John 11:1
Jesus Journeys to Jerusalem	Mt 20:17; Mk 10:32; Lk 18:31
The Jewish Council Plots Jesus' Death	Mt 26:3; Jn 11:47
Jesus' Arrival at Bethany	John 12:1
Jesus Enters Jerusalem	Mt 21:1; Mk 11:1; Lk 19:29; Jn 12:12
Jesus Cleanses the Temple	Mt 21:12; Mk 11:15; Lk 19:45
Jesus Teaches in the Temple	Mt 21:23; Mk 1:27; Lk 20:1
Judas' Treacherous Plot	Mt 26:14; Mk 4:10; Lk 22:3

Tuesday-The Last Week of Jesus' Life

Preparation for the Passover	Mt 26:17; Mk14:12; Lk 22:7
The Supper of the Last Evening	Mt 26:20; Mk 14:7; Lk 22:14
Jesus Washes His Disciples' Feet	John 13:1
The Betrayer Revealed	John 13:10
Jesus' Last Discourses to His Disciples	Jn 13:31; Jn 17
Jesus Institutes "The Lord's Supper"	Mt 26:26; Mk 22; Lk 22:19

140

| Peter's Three Denials Foretold | Mt 26:34; Mk 14:30; Lk 22:34; Jn 13:38 |
| Jesus' Agony in Gethsemane | Mt 26:36; Mk 14:32; Lk 22:39; Jn 18:1 |

Wednesday Morning: Please Note:

In order for the events to occur in the manner that is recorded in the Bible there is no verse which states that Jesus was crucified on a Friday. However, there are no less then four (4) references which say He must be in the tomb for three days (Mat 16:21). The full Biblical account to support this thought is recorded as the last subject in this work.

Sometime Between 6:00PM(the night before) and 6:00 AM

The Betrayal and Arrest	Mt 26:47; Mk 14:43; Lk 22:47; Jn 18:2
Jesus Taken to Annas	John 18:13
Before Caiaphas the High Priest	Mt 26:57; Mk 14:53; Lk 22:54; Jn 18:19
Peter's Three Denials	Mt 26:69; Mk 14:66; Lk 22:54; Jn 18:15
Jesus Before the Jewish Council	Mt 27:1; Mk 15:1; Lk 22:66

The next events occur between 6:00 AM and 9:00 AM (the 3rd hour)

Jesus Before Pilate	Mt 27:2,11; Mk 15:1; Lk 23:1; Jn 18:28
Pilate Declares Jesus Innocent	Lk 23:4; Jn 19:4
Pilate Sends Jesus to Herod	Luke 23:7
The Jews Reject Jesus	Mt 27:21, 25; Mk 15:6; Lk 23:18; Jn 18:40, 19:15
Pilate Condemns Jesus to Death	Mt 27:26; Mk 15:15; Lk 23:24; Jn 19:16
Jesus Mocked by the Soldiers	Mt 27:27; Mk 15:16; Jn 19:2
Jesus Led Away to be Crucified	Mt 27:31; Mk 15:20; Lk 23:33; Jn 19:18

The Crucifixion took place at the 3rd hour (Mk 15:25)

The Crucifixion of Jesus	Mt 27:35; Lk 23:33; Jn 19:18
Jesus on the Cross	Mt 27:36; Mk 15:25; Jn 19:19
Dividing of Jesus' Clothes	Mark 15:24
Jesus' Prayer of Intercession	Luke 23:34
Insults From Ordinary People	Mat 27:39-40
Mocked By Chief Priests	Mark 15:31
Mocked by Soldiers	Luke 23:36-37
Insults From One Criminal on Cross	Luke 23:39
Rebuke by the Other Criminal	Luke 23:40, 42
Answer from Jesus	Luke 23:43
Jesus Speaks to Mother and Disciple	John 19:26-27

From the 6th to the 9th hours (12 Noon to 3 PM)

Darkness Over the Land for Three Hours	Mark 15:33
Jesus Cries Out	Mat 27:46
Jesus Given Vinegar to Drink	John 19:28
Jesus Declares, "It Is Finished"	John 19:30
Jesus Gives Up His Spirit	Luke 23:46
Death of Jesus	Mt 27:50; Mk 15:37

Events Immediately Following Jesus' Death

Tearing of the Temple Curtain	Mat 27:51
Tombs Break Open	Mat 27:52
The Centurion's Witness	Mt 27:54; Mk 15:39; Lk 23:47
Confession of the Multitude	Luke 23:48
Thieves Legs Broken	John 19:31-32
Soldiers Pierce Jesus' Side	John 19:34
The Burial of Jesus	Mt 27:57; Mk 15:42; Lk 23:50; Jn 19:38
Sealing of the Tomb	Mat 27:66
The Resurrection of Jesus	Mt 28:1; Mk 16:1; Lk 24:1; Jn 20:1

Appearances of Jesus After the Resurrection

To Mary Magdalene	Mk 16:9; Jn 20:11
To the Women	Mat 28:1
To the Eleven	Mk 16:14, Jn 20:19
To Two Going to Emmaus	Mk 16:12; Lk 24:13
To the Eleven (a week later)	John 20:26
To the Apostles in Galilee	Mk 16:14, Jn 21:1
To Peter	Lk 24:34; 1 Cor 15:5
To Five Hundred Brethren in Galilee	1 Cor 15:6
To James	1 Cor 15:7
To Paul	1 Cor 15:8
Jesus' Commission to the Apostles	Mt 28:19; Mk 16:15; Lk 24:44
Jesus Talks With Peter	John 21:15
The Ascension of Jesus	Mk 16:19; Lk 24:50; Acts 1:4
The Descent of God as the Holy Spirit	Acts 2:1

The Miracles

The First Miracle: Water Made Wine	John 2:1
Many Healings	Mt 4:23, 8:16, 15:30; Mk 1:32; Lk 4:40; etc.
A Leper	Mt 8:1-4; Mk 1:40; Lk 5:12
The Centurion's Servant	Mt 8:5; Lk 7:1
Peter's Mother-in-Law	Mt 8:14; Mk 1:29; Lk 4:38
The Tempest Stilled	Mt 8:23; Mk 4:35; Lk 8:22
Two Demoniacs	Mt 8:28; Mk 5:1; Lk 8:26
A Palsied Man	Mt 9:1; Mk 2:1; Lk 5:18
The Twelve-Year Afflicted Woman	Mt 9:20; Mk 5:25; Lk 8:43

Raising of Jairus' Daughter	Mt 9:23; Mk 5:22; Lk 8:41
Two Blind Men	Mat 9:27
A Dumb Demoniac	Mat 9:32, 12:22; Luke 14
A Man With a Withered Hand	Mt 12:10; Mk 3:1; Lk 6:6
Five Thousand Fed	Mt 14:15; Mk 6:35; Lk 9:12; Jn 6:1
Jesus Walks on the Sea	Mt 14:22; Mk 6:47; Jn 6:16
The Syrophenician's Daughter	Mt 15:21; Mk 7:24
Four Thousand Fed	Mt 15:32; Mk 8:1
The Epileptic Boy	Mt 17:14; Mk 9:14; Lk 9:37
Two Blind Men (Jerico)	Mat 20:30
A Man With an Unclean Spirit	Mk 1:23; Lk 4:33
A Deaf Mute	Mark 7:31
A Blind Man (Bethesda)	Mark 8:22
Blind Bartimaeus	Mt 20:30; Mk 10:46; Lk 18:35
Great Amount of Fishes	Luke 5:4
Raising of Widow's Son	Luke 7:11
An Infirm Woman	Luke 13:11
A Dropsical Man	Luke 14:1
Ten Lepers	Luke 17:11
Malchus' Ear Healed	Luke 22:50
A Nobleman's Son	John 4:46
A Cripple (Bethesda)	John 5:1
A Man Born Blind	John 9:1
Raising of Lazarus	John 11:38
A Great Haul of Fishes	John 21:1

The Parables

The Builders	Mt 7:24-27; Lk 6:47-49
The Sower	Mt 13:3; Mk 4:1; Lk 8:4
The Wheat and the Tares	Mat 13:24-30

The Mustard Seed	Mt 13:31; Mk 4:30; Lk 13:18
The Leaven	Mt 13:33; Lk 13:20
The Hidden Treasure	Mat 13:44
The Pearl of Great Price	Mat 13:45
The Net	Mat 13:47
The Unmerciful Servant	Mat 18:23-35
The Laborers in the Vineyard	Mat 20:1-16
The Two Sons	Mat 21:28-32
The Wicked Husbandmen	Mat 21:33-46; Luke 20:9-18
The Marriage Feast	Mat 22:1-14
The Fig Tree	Mat 24:32
The Ten Virgins	Mat 25:1-13
The Talents	Mat 25:14-30
The Seed Growing Secretly	Mark 4:26-29
The Good Samaritan	Luke 10:25-37
The Rich Fool	Luke 12:13-21
The Fruitless Fig Tree	Luke 13:6-9
The Great Supper	Luke 14:16-24
On Counting the Cost	Luke 14:25-33
The Lost Sheep	Luke 15:3-7
The Lost Coin	Luke 15:8-10
The Lost Son	Luke 15:11-32
The Dishonest Steward	Luke 16:1-14
The Rich Man and Lazarus	Luke 16:19-31
The Importunate Widow and Unjust Judge	Luke 18:1-8
The Pharisee and Publican	Luke 18:8-14
The Pounds	Luke 19:11-27

The Three Days Jesus Was In The Tomb

The following is a study to encourage thought, it is not meant to cause doubt or for you to change your ideas about Good Friday or Easter Sunday. However, as an American we normally do not follow other nations' holidays and yet we are dealing with Jewish holidays, being Passover and the Feast of Unleavened Bread, leading up to the crucifixion. Tradition

has entered and surrounds the term sabbath as used in the crucifixion account; without taking into consideration Jewish customs. Using the Old Testament the history and manner for following Jewish customs on these holidays should be available for us to study. In doing this there would also be information whereby there can be a full three days that Jesus was in the tomb.

Here's the Biblical text to support Jesus' own statement in Mat 12:40.

The first thing for us to look at is that there must be a full three days to account for within text. The following four references show that the mention of three days is made in more then one place.

Matthew 12:40 (KJV) For as Jonas was three days and three nights in the whale's belly; so shall the Son of man be three days and three nights in the heart of the earth.

Matthew 16:21 (KJV) From that time forth began Jesus to show unto his disciples, how that he must go unto Jerusalem, and suffer many things of the elders and chief priests and scribes, and be killed, and be raised again the third day.

Matthew 27:62-63 (KJV) Now the next day, that followed the day of the preparation, the chief priests and Pharisees came together unto Pilate, {63} Saying, Sir, we remember that that deceiver said, while he was yet alive, After three days I will rise again.

Mark 8:31 (KJV) And he began to teach them, that the Son of man must suffer many things, and be rejected of the elders, and of the chief priests, and scribes, and be killed, and after three days rise again.

What must be shown so you can understand that this actually is fulfilled by Biblical account? There seems to be great confusion over the use of the term Sabbath that is used for the resurrection of Jesus. Let's first look at the account leading to Jesus' crucifixion.

Mark 15:42 (KJV) And now when the even was come, because

it was the preparation, that is, the day before the sabbath,
John 19:14 (KJV) And it was the preparation of the passover, and about the sixth hour: and he saith unto the Jews, Behold your King!
John 19:31 (KJV) The Jews therefore, because it was the preparation, that the bodies should not remain upon the cross on the sabbath day, (for that sabbath day was an high day,) besought Pilate that their legs might be broken, and that they might be taken away.

Notice in these three verses the use of the term preparation and also in verse 31 that this was a high day. In reading Matthew, Mark, Luke and John there is no mention of the weekly Sabbath as being a high day or that there is a preparation day before the weekly Sabbath; therefore, this must be a different Sabbath day, and if so, must be supportable by Biblical text. Consider what is customary in our time. We do not call every day a holiday. A holiday is a special day. Look again at verse 31above at the use of the term high day.

Let's look at text which supports different days, other then the weekly Sabbath, that are called Sabbath days.
Numbers 28:16-18 (KJV) And in the fourteenth day of the first month is the passover of the LORD. {17} And in the fifteenth day of this month is the feast: seven days shall unleavened bread be eaten. {18} In the first day shall be an holy convocation; ye shall do no manner of servile work therein:
Leviticus 23:3-8 (KJV) Six days shall work be done: but the seventh day is the sabbath of rest, an holy convocation; ye shall do no work therein: it is the sabbath of the LORD in all your dwellings. {4} These are the feasts of the LORD, even holy convocations, which ye shall proclaim in their seasons. {5} In the fourteenth day of the first month at even is the Lord's passover. {6} And on the fifteenth day of the same month is the feast of unleavened bread unto the LORD: seven days ye must eat unleavened bread. {7} In the first day ye shall have an holy convocation: ye shall do no servile work

therein. {8} But ye shall offer an offering made by fire unto the LORD seven days: in the seventh day is an holy convocation: ye shall do no servile work therein.

First notice in verse three of Leviticus 23 the day of rest is called a Sabbath, this is the weekly Sabbath. Understand that the terms Sabbath and holy convocation are synonymous. Notice also, in verse five the fourteenth day of the first month. Now go back to Numbers 28:18 and insert Sabbath instead of holy convocation, the meaning would remain the same.

Leviticus 23:24 (KJV) Speak unto the children of Israel, saying, In the seventh month, in the first day of the month, shall ye have a sabbath, a memorial of blowing of trumpets, an holy convocation.

Leviticus 23:27 (KJV) Also on the tenth day of this seventh month there shall be a day of atonement: it shall be an holy convocation unto you; and ye shall afflict your souls, and offer an offering made by fire unto the LORD.

Leviticus 23:32 (KJV) It shall be unto you a sabbath of rest, and ye shall afflict your souls: in the ninth day of the month at even, from even unto even, shall ye celebrate your sabbath.

Lev 23:32 is one of the keys that will help define the day Jesus was crucified. Notice that the day, or Sabbath, goes from even unto even. That would be from twilight (dusk) until twilight the next day, or in present day terms from 6:00PM until 6:00PM the next day.

Leviticus 23:34 (KJV) Speak unto the children of Israel, saying, The fifteenth day of this seventh month shall be the feast of tabernacles for seven days unto the LORD. {35} On the first day shall be an holy convocation: ye shall do no servile work therein. {36} Seven days ye shall offer an offering made by fire unto the LORD: on the eight day shall be an holy convocation unto you; and ye shall offer an offering made by fire unto the LORD: it is a solemn assembly; and ye shall do no servile work therein. {37} These are the feasts of the LORD,

which ye shall proclaim to be holy convocations, to offer an offering made by fire unto the LORD, a burnt offering, and a meat offering, a sacrifice, and drink offerings, every thing upon his day:

You should now understand that a high day would be a feast day, a holy convocation or a Sabbath day.

In Numbers 28:16 and Leviticus 23:5 there is the term fourteenth day of the first month. Let's show what day this is in a different manner. Text above identifies that the fourteenth is the LORD's passover. Where does this come from and how do we identify the Jewish month?
Exodus 12:1-6 (KJV) And the LORD spake unto Moses and Aaron in the land of Egypt, saying, {2} This month shall be unto you the beginning of months: it shall be the first month of the year to you. {3} Speak ye unto all the congregation of Israel, saying, In the tenth day of this month they shall take to them every man a lamb, according to the house of their fathers, a lamb for an house: {4} And if the household be too little for the lamb, let him and his neighbour next unto his house take it according to the number of the souls; every man according to his eating shall make your count for the lamb. {5} Your lamb shall be without blemish, a male of the first year: ye shall take it out from the sheep, or from the goats: {6} And ye shall keep it up until the fourteenth day of the same month: and the whole assembly of the congregation of Israel shall kill it in the evening.

Notice the time the lamb is killed ... in the evening. The following verse will identify which Jewish month we are talking about.
Esther 3:7 (KJV) In the first month, that is, the month Nisan, ...

Most any good concordance will transpose Nisan into the month we call April.

In the account from Exodus we have a lamb which is to be scarified. Look at what John the Baptist says about Jesus in the following verse.

John 1:29 (KJV) The next day John seeth Jesus coming unto him, and saith, Behold the Lamb of God, which taketh away the sin of the world.

Here we have the true sacrifice that God sent to correct the error caused by Adam. We also know that the sacrifice had to take place on the preparation day, or fourteenth of Nisan, before the Sabbath Feast of Unleavened Bread and that a Jewish day went from evening to evening. Therefore, it would seem to me that the crucifixion and burial of Jesus had to take place on Wednesday prior to twilight. You would then have Wednesday night, Thursday day, Thursday night, Friday day, Friday night and Saturday day which would make up three days and three nights before the beginning of the first day of the week which would be Saturday at evening (twilight or about 6:00PM). Then the following verse would be correct to complete the Biblical account.

Matthew 28:1-6 (KJV) In the end of the sabbath, as it began to dawn toward the first day of the week, came Mary Magdalene and the other Mary to see the sepulchre. {2} And, behold, there was a great earthquake: for the angel of the Lord descended from heaven, and came and rolled back the stone from the door, and sat upon it. {3} His countenance was like lightning, and his raiment white as snow: {4} And for fear of him the keepers did shake, and became as dead men. {5} And the angel answered and said unto the women, Fear not ye: for I know that ye seek Jesus, which was crucified. {6} He is not here: for he is risen, as he said. Come, see the place where the Lord lay.

We read in Leviticus 23:32 that the day started at evening

and went until the next evening. The actual resurrection of Jesus occurred sometime between twilight on Saturday (end of the Sabbath and beginning of the first day) and the coming of dawn on Sunday. The reason the stone was rolled away was not to let Jesus out but to let the others in. Jesus was already resurrected by the time the two Marys arrived at dawn.

Remember it is not the death of Jesus that gives the free gift from God, it is His resurrection that provides this gift.

Where did tradition enter that could have possibly changed the meaning? Historically, we tend to forget that common man did not have the Holy Bible until 1611 when the King James version was printed. Up to that date the Bible remained, for the most part, in the hands of the church and the nobility. The church, or the influence from the nobility upon the church, could establish any number of ideas which would become tradition. There was no check made by common man to see if what was being said was true, or even accurate.

Now days, it is most difficult to change these traditions even when the Bible itself indicates otherwise.

Read your Bible to understand and know the truth as it is recorded.

Forth coming release!

God's Heritage Chart©™

Forget the begots of the King James Bible. This 58X40 inch full color chart visually illustrates the 75 generations of mankind from Adam to Jesus (as recorded in the Bible). Over 1550 entries with each referenced by a Biblical verse. The most thorough genealogy chart available for Bible Study. Simply stated, **"A picture is worth a thousand words"**. See the relationship of major Bible characters. All the sons of Abraham are identified and shown. There is a separate colored area for each of the twelve tribes of Israel and one for Ishmael. Fully indexed with grid coordinates to ease location of each person.

God's Heritage Chart Companion©

A must for anyone interested in Bible study! Starts where God's Heritage Chart stops. While each name on the chart has a Bible reference the chart cannot list all references pertaining to each individual. The companion gives the full verses for each name on the chart so you can read and see who these people are. Also, there is a cross reference for different spellings of the names between the NIV and NKJV. However, that is not all. Learn the humor of the *ites*. View the list of the kings for Judah and Israel. Finally, there's a chapter called "Did You Know?", which shows some of the more unusual recordings from the King James Bible.

See *You* at the book signing!